THE LEGACY

YESTERDAY'S SPIRITUAL LESSONS FOR
TODAY'S SPIRIT-LED CHRISTIAN

CATHERINE GREEN

Kingdom Publishers

Copyright© Catherine Green 2024

All rights reserved. No part of this book may be reproduced in any form by photocopying or any electronic or mechanical means, including information storage or retrieval systems, without permission in writing from both the copyright owner and the publisher of the book. The right of Catherine Green to be identified as the author of this work has been asserted by her in accordance with the Copyright, Designs and Patents Act 1988 and any subsequent amendments thereto.

A catalogue record for this book is available from the British Library.

All scripture quotations have been taken from the New International version of the Bible

ISBN: 978-1-916801-09-7

1st Edition 2024 by Kingdom Publishers, London, UK.

You can purchase copies of this book from any leading bookstore or at www.kingdompublishers.co.uk

Dedicated to my wonderful family...with love

Contents

Acknowledgements	9
Foreword	10
PART ONE William's Story	11
New Life	13
Spiritual Awakening	20
New Beginnings	28
Growing	37
Minister in the Making	44
Home is Where the Heart is	54
Fighting the Good Fight	59
The Finishing Line	65
PART TWO Catherine's Story	73
New Life	75
Spiritual Awakening	80
New Beginnings with One Foot in the World	86
Growing	94
PART THREE God's Legacy Lessons	103
Legacy Lesson One Relationship not Religion	108
Legacy Lesson Two The Gift of Grace	112
Legacy Lesson Three Milk or Maturity?	116
Legacy Lesson Four Prayer, Privilege and Power	121
Legacy Lesson Five Money Matters	126
Legacy Lesson Six Working Well	131
Legacy Lesson Seven Guard the Gospel	137
Legacy Lesson Eight Heart or Hand?	142
Epilogue	145
Bibliography	146

Acknowledgements

A very big thank you to Rose Marie and Phil for all your support and unconditional love throughout the writing of this book. Your patience, expertise and advice have been a tremendous blessing. I could not have done it without you!

Thanks also go to my special dad for giving me a lifetime love of reading, history and genealogy.

Thank you to Gail, my faithful friend and sister in Christ, for your constant reassurance and listening ear.

I am very grateful to the staff at the Buckinghamshire records office, whose help over the years has been invaluable.

Many thanks also go to Long Crendon Baptist Church, both for the warm welcome and encouragement and also for the precious gift of William's marble tablet, which has a special place in my garden.

Foreword

This is a saga bridging two centuries. It is a tale of family, friends and foes; poverty and provision; faith and fortitude; plans and purpose. It speaks of lessons to be learnt, minds that are mended and hearts that are healed. This is a story about connection and love: God's unfailing love for us.

It is an account of the life of my great, great, great, great grandfather, William Hopcraft; some of it told in his own words. It is also a narrative of my journey as a Christian, as I weaved together the spiritual lessons *handed down* to me.

When researching my family tree, I discovered more than names and dates on headstones. I uncovered a treasured thread of bloodline history. It was the missing piece of a jigsaw that I had been looking for. It made the picture complete. God used a passion of mine, to perfect a healing in me and to bring me into the fullness of His grace.

Although narrated as a story, this is a true account of William's life and a true report of my journey so far. More importantly, God's truth runs throughout, as a beacon of light, carried from age to age. The historical and emotional descriptions are based on knowledge, personal experience and, at times, my imagination.

Now that the preamble is over it's time to introduce you to my 4th great grandfather William Hopcraft and tell you about the legacy lessons left on a shelf for nearly two hundred years.

PART ONE
William's Story

New Life

It was a spring day, the season of new life and fresh beginnings, when William's lungs took their first breath and he cried his first cry. He was Robert and Ann's first boy, a son, who would learn to walk and work in the footsteps of his father. Ann did not tarry in bed for long; not for her were the privileges afforded to the ladies of society. She had water to fetch, food to cook and a house to clean. She also had to care for Annie, who at two years old, was too young to understand the impact her new brother was about to make on the family.

Every night, once the children were asleep, Ann would begin her evening shift. Sitting near the window, a single tallow candle her only source of light, she deftly, moved the bobbins across her work. Twisting and plaiting the fine thread, creating luxurious lace to adorn dresses that she could only ever dream of wearing.

Ann knew that William's future seemed bleak. He had been born into an unrelenting cycle of poverty, with no way out. His surroundings were crude and sparse but not in a romantic 'baby in the manger' way. There was no luxury in the place they called home. It was small, dark and draughty.

An old homemade wooden table took central place with two hard upright chairs providing their only form of comfort. The straw-filled bed was low and rough and the only pillow they possessed was the one on which she used to make her lace. Food was a daily challenge, sometimes they had enough to fill their rumbling bellies and other days they felt sick with hunger; the type of hunger that twists your stomach until it feels like it is eating itself. The outlook for their lives was grim. Ann was aware that there was little potential for change but as she looked into her son's innocent eyes, she dared to have a glimmer of hope that a better life lay ahead.

The Hopcraft family were not unique to the situation in which they found themselves. They were in the same economically sinking boat as most of their neighbours. They muddled through but the anxieties and concerns of hardship etched their way into the lines on their faces. The poverty trap had caught them and they were ensnared in its grasp. Ann thought about a different life. She imagined herself with enough food on the table and clean soft clothes against her children's skin. She thought about them growing up and who they would become. She reflected on all that was to come; the next ten years, the next twenty years but she never anticipated the influence and inspiration her son would be in two hundred and forty years' time.

She had no idea that her William would one day leave an inheritance that would reach through the generations, to touch the heart of his great, great, great, great granddaughter. They did not have an inkling... but God knew.

William was born on Thursday 18th April 1776 and the legacy, that would take many years to reach its fulfilment, had already been established. God always has a plan!

Eight days later, on the Friday, the family spruced themselves up and walked the mile journey to their parish church, to get their newest arrival baptised. The high stone tower and fourteenth century architecture of the church of St Nicholas dominated the east end of the village of Long Crendon. It was dimly lit and chilly inside, with memorial slabs, set into the grey stone floor, marking the graves of well-known villagers. It housed a timeworn pulpit, old tombs and a number of scruffy wooden pews. The family stood quietly, waiting, in the shadows, for the vicar to call them forward towards the font. Their insignificance emphasised by an extraordinary oversized pew, set aside for the rich and honoured among the congregation. It rose above them, to ten feet high, dwarfing them with its lofty attitude.

The church was obliged to open its doors to this ordinary little family. They were without wealth or social standing, but child mortality was high and the parish church had a duty to baptise infants by the second Sunday following their birth.

As Ann anticipated William's christening, she held him tight, tenderly stroking his head before tracing a finger down his rosy cheek. He was perfect. Just like the others had been. Thoughts of two more beautiful babies intruded into her mind, along with the unwanted images of them in their tiny makeshift coffins; pale grey skin contrasting against their black woollen shrouds. Mary and Elizabeth had never reached the age of three. She had fed, nurtured and loved them and then they were gone; flickering flames blown out by a harsh cold wind, leaving an indelible shadow on the wall of Ann's heart. Now she had another new life to take care of and despite the euphoria of his birth, doubts and fears for his future were creeping in.

Once they were called to the front of the font, the event was quick and functional with no pomp or ceremony. William's head was sprinkled, a few words spoken and a fee of one shilling and six pence was hurriedly received and recorded.

Peace of mind, for Ann and Robert, came at a financial but worthwhile cost. If their newborn was to die, at least he had been presented to God and baptised in the name of the Father, the Son and the Holy Spirit. It was a dedication of a type and unbeknown to them, a precursor of things to come.

Within the next five years, Ann had two more sons. They named their second son Robert, after his father, and then came their third son Richard. It was a difficult birth. Ann's natural relief, as her son was born, quickly turned to tragic sorrow as she stared down at his lifeless body.

As she walked to the graveyard, an all-encompassing sadness enveloped her. The devastating feeling of loss was an emotion that she had become accustomed to but it was felt no less keenly than that of her first two children. In her world, the death of a child was commonplace. She had borne six children and buried three. Her heart was half-empty but the harshness of her life left no time for the freedom of public grief. She had to lay to rest the face of her sadness. She concealed it in the earth along with her son. There was work to be done.

There were no more babies for Robert and Ann. They continued to live, work and raise their young family in Long Crendon, a small village in Buckinghamshire, England. They came from Crendon stock and this was their home. Their parents and grandparents before them had lived the same tough, meagre lives; an unyielding circle of trying to make short ends meet.

They lived on the east edge of the parish in a cottage nearby the site of Notley Abbey; an Augustinian abbey, founded in the 12th century that had suffered the ravages of the dissolution of the monasteries in 1539 by the hands of Henry the Eighth. All that endured, as a shadow of the monastic community, was a miserable old farmhouse and a few remnants of the cloisters that now formed cow stalls. The river Thames ran close by and a relic from the days of the monks, an old water mill remained, with overgrown reed-filled fishponds and a smell of stagnant water. This was William's playground, his little feet squelching in the soaked soil, where men of faith had once toiled the land.

Their home was not a quintessential English rose covered country cottage with a vegetable garden and sweet peas growing in a pot by the door. It was a small, basic, dilapidated dwelling, with no running water or sanitation. The whole family lived and slept in one room, with a small back scullery where Robert plied his trade. There was no expectation of privacy for any of them. Ann rose early every morning to clear out the embers, from the night before and, if they had enough fuel, light a new fire for the day ahead. Water was fetched, in a bucket, from a village well, and chamber-pots emptied of their slops and vigorously scrubbed.

Their living conditions were appalling. The winter days were, damp, dark, and often cold with animal-fat-spitting candles their only night-time form of light. The fire, when they had one, was both a curse and a blessing. The warmth from the orange flames a welcome relief from the biting chill in the air but the smoke that filled the room made everything smell of ash. On a bad day, it would cover the whole room in a dusting of soot. Ann had to keep her precious lace wrapped up in linen and stored in the back in an old wooden box. Dirty lace meant no sale. It was better to be cold and be able to work than to be warm and starve.

Ann conjured up hot meals for her family in a large black pot, hung on a metal rail over the fire. Vegetables in watery gravy, served with bread, was their standard fare with mutton stew as a tasty rare treat when life was looking up.

The outdoor days of summer were something to look forward to. They could clear their lungs, taking long, deep, breaths to fill them with fresh air. Ann and the other women in the neighbourhood sat outside and let the sun add a blush to their sallow faces as they chatted together, all the while creating beautiful designs in lace. The sunshine brought more freedom for the children and the sound of their laughter as they played together was a welcome noise after the silence of winter.

William's childhood was already mapped out. His lot in life was to live in wretched poverty with no formal education or any perceptible prospect of ever achieving anything better. He grew up in the village surrounded by lace makers, agricultural workers and needle producers. When he was able to start work, at the age of five, one of the jobs on offer was to earn a few pennies by kicking a sand filled hessian bag of newly formed needles up and down the dusty streets of the village. His small feet and thin legs working with all the enthusiasm and energy of youth until the needles were smooth and polished. Everyone had to work as soon as they were capable of doing something.

His father, Robert, was a tailor. He made ordinary hand-sewn clothes, out of coarse woollen material for anyone that could afford to buy from him. It was a skilled but slow process, with little remuneration and few regular customers. Most people in his circle only owned the clothes they stood in, with a few possessing a *Sunday best* outfit, and so repeat custom was difficult to maintain.

William was destined to follow in his father's footsteps and from a small child he was taught to master the tools of the trade. Before he reached the age of ten, his nimble fingers and young eyes had become expert at threading needles, tying knots, and tacking the thick material together. There was no school for William, everything that he learnt as a boy was taught to him by his father. He grew up without any advantages, without any money, with very little food, no formal education and with hardly any possessions.

Despite always fighting against the odds, he survived childhood and avoided the awful diseases of typhus, cholera and smallpox that could run rampant throughout the village. He grew in stature and regardless of, or maybe because of the deprivation he suffered, he grew into a caring and conscientious young man.

William did not expect his life to change but when he was twelve, something happened that would alter the direction of his days forever. His father at the age of forty-seven, succumbed to the trials and hardships of his life and without warning passed away. William was shocked and devastated; the man who had been there for him his whole life, the man who had taught him all that he knew, had left him. The family walked the familiar path to the graveyard, huddled together, weary with worry and fraught with sorrow. Robert's death had left a gaping hole in their hearts as well as in their pockets. He had left behind a grieving widow and three growing children. Who would take care of them now?

Despite his tender years, William knew that he had to assume responsibility for those he loved. His mother needed him to be strong, for his sister Annie as well as his younger brother, Robert. He had to step up to be the *man of the house*. The weight settled heavily on his small shoulders. It was a burden that was hard to bear but he faced it with courage and determination. The characteristics that he displayed in the face of loss and hardship were to grow and mature in him throughout his life. Unbeknown to him, he was being shaped on the anvil of change and refined in the flames of the forge. He was being prepared!

In the last few weeks of his life, because of the heavy workload, Robert had begun training a new apprentice. He was a diligent young man, older than William and more experienced in the art of tailoring. He offered to stay on and help the family run the business as much as he could in the hope that the little cottage industry could stay afloat and support them all. Ann continued with her lacework, but their income was still minimal. William wrote that *'they were left in a condition of great destitution.'* Rent had to be paid first and they were *'often much distressed from want of food.'*

A condition of great destitution was a distressing situation to be in. Food was scarce. They were desperate, deprived, miserable and hungry! The most important thing to pay for was a roof over their heads. If they could not pay the landlord his dues, then they would be out on the street with nowhere to go. The situation of living a slice of bread away from starvation continued for several years. Their stomachs became hollow and their limbs thin for want of a morsel of meat.

When William was sixteen, his sister married. With this turn of events, the dynamics of the family changed and he decided to take over the running his father's business solely by himself. This turned out to be more difficult than he had first imagined. William did not find the art of tailoring something that came naturally to him. In his own words, '*he wasn't that good at it.*' His father had passed away before he could teach him all the tricks and skills of the profession but William persevered until he was able to tailor to a reasonable standard. Now he was running the business; dealing with clients, buying materials, making garments, selling and managing the money and it was especially hard because he could neither read nor write.

William was motivated. He wanted the business to be a success. He desperately wanted to provide for his mother and make life easier for the family. He was determined to do better but knew that he was lacking in the basics of learning. He understood what was required of him, and out of this, the desire to become educated was born. He set himself the task of learning to read and write, requesting help from anyone with the willingness, knowledge and time to reveal to him the wonder of words. It was not an easy road, but after many months of laborious work, he succeeded and became proficient in both skills. It was a wonderful achievement.

His new talents opened up a new world for him. Now that he could read and write, everything was much easier, particularly when it came to the family business. On a social and political level, local pamphlets and newspapers became fascinating sources of information. All of which enabled him to relate to people with a new perspective and comprehension. Unbeknown to him he had just accomplished a key stage in God's design for his life. Learning to write was not only a skill for his personal benefit but it was to be a gift that God intended to use for many years, even beyond William's own lifetime.

Spiritual Awakening

Despite William's hard work, the business was not an overnight success. He was impatient for a breakthrough but, regardless of all his endeavours, it did not come. He felt he was failing and before long the proverbial black dog started snapping at his heels. He became depressed and anxious in his struggle to make a living for the family. He had tried all he humanly could to make a positive change but to no avail. This was a dark time in William's life, a time when he was ready to give in and give up. That is, until one noteworthy night when God made His presence known.

William was lying on his bed, mulling things over, when a powerful thought came into his head. He realised that God was there and that *He* could help. He had a strong impression that God could and would intervene on his and the family's behalf, and provide for their needs. William was beginning to see the world through spiritual eyes. He turned towards the wall, as if in search of a private moment with His Creator, and prayed that God would cause him to have '*plenty of work and prosper his labours.*' He did not ask for a financial gift from a miraculous benefactor. He did not want a hand out. He wanted a hand up. He was asking God to bless his work.

It was a simple heart-felt prayer and William did not have to wait long for God to answer. Throughout the following month, the trade in his business began to increase. More people came to his door. More orders were taken. More money came in. At the same time, his brother, Robert, who was now fifteen, and had previously been a lace maker alongside his mother, asked if he could also learn the trade of tailoring. William, the apprentice, had now become the teacher. Robert was already dextrous thanks to his lace making and was soon creating quality clothes alongside William. With more funds coming in, things began to look up for the Hopcraft family. Food was no longer a scarcity; they had meat to eat and bread on the table; the pangs of physical hunger began to ease.

Feeling more confident and not so tied down by the rigours of impoverishment, William began to mingle with society more and began to ring the changes. He knew that God had helped him and so he began to consider formal religion as *'necessary and advantageous'* in his life, even though he had no proper concept of its true nature. He started to attend the church where he had been baptised, praying, taking the sacraments and singing in the choir. It was a place where rules and regulations reigned and the only place, in his small world, where he could catch a glimpse of God.

When William partook in Holy Communion, he had no real understanding of the significance of the sacraments that were offered to him. For him it was a ritual; available to those who had been baptised and confirmed. Religion along with its trappings and ties became important to him. He was searching for the truth outside of himself. He was looking to an institution and not to the conviction of Christ within.

In listening to sermons, William became conscious of his behaviour and framed his conduct within his understanding of biblical principals; doing his best to *'refrain from any outward acts of evil.'* This was a tall order and he was tough on himself. A raised voice or a moment of irritation and he had missed the mark. Each time he failed, he felt the weight of sin and full of grief was compelled to start all over again. For William there was judgement and condemnation in his newfound religion. He spent his days trying to reach perfection, in his own strength, but by sunset, his efforts had always fallen short. He had grasped the principles of the *law* but had not understood the grace and love that Jesus offered. William was a serious minded seventeen-year-old and did not give up easily. His determination was a characteristic that would benefit him greatly in his adult life, but for now, it resulted in personal disapproval and judgement.

For three years, he continued with his misunderstanding and confusion, a constant battle against his flesh. The struggle was not made any easier when he fell in love with a beautiful girl. Their courtship was brief. He asked for her hand in marriage and she said yes! Another young couple: ready to tie the knot that would bind their lives together. Things were about to change, but in ways that William could never have imagined.

Mary Fryer was two years William's senior, a lace maker from the same village. They made their vows before God and before a congregation of friends and family on Thursday 16th June 1796. Love and laughter was in the air as they emerged from the inner dimness of the church into the brightness of the day and an unknown future.

William's life with his new love began. They moved to a small house on the High Street in the centre of the village. They still had to work hard but it was a positive time, an exciting time of growing together. William was happy but he was still searching for a deeper meaning to his life. Although by no means rich, their combined incomes made everyday living slightly more comfortable. They had regular, nutritious food on the table and William began to think less about food for his stomach and more about sustenance for his soul.

He had no doubt that God had heard him that night, when he was sixteen, and had prayed for help. However, he wrongly believed that God was a strict disciplinarian with a list of rules to be followed. William spent his time adhering to the *letter of the law* in order to be acceptable in God's sight.

The state church in the late eighteenth century was often more political than religious and catered mainly for the rich and influential. Most of the interest in religion, by the upper echelons of society, was only theoretical. William, on the other hand, was looking for reality and deep spiritual truths.

As siblings, William and his brother, Robert, were close but in terms of personalities, they were complete opposites. William had carried much of the responsibility, since his father's death and as a result was a serious young man. The more fun-loving Robert did not understand his brother's new way of life. It was irritating and he often took to criticising William; making fun of him for being too pious. William was sincere but sanctimonious, with a holier than thou attitude that did little to endear him to others.

Ironically, it was through his brother that William ultimately stepped down from delusion to be able to walk in the truth.

Robert, despite his determination to ignore William's religious words, had come under conviction of his own sin. His brother's piousness had been so dominant and so persuasive that he too became aware of God, and like William, believed that God was a heavenly being that demanded perfect behaviour. He had such little knowledge that he quickly came to the wrong conclusion that he had committed an unpardonable sin against the Holy Ghost.

This was a serious transgression. Blasphemy against the Holy Spirit is an intentional, hard-edged, determined defiance and opposition to the truth of the Spirit. It turns a person's heart to stone. It is the one thing that cannot be forgiven.

Not understanding, Robert believed that because of his attitude to religion he had come under the judgement of God.

The poor boy was so distressed that he sought help and comfort from the one person who he thought would have answers, his brother. William however, knew nothing of the saving principles of the Gospel and even less about what it really meant to blaspheme the Holy Spirit. In his naivety, William gave the best advice he could but it was without any real conviction or reassurance.

This dilemma was enough of a catalyst for Robert to start searching out the truth for himself. He had become aware of a man who was preaching in Thame, a village about four miles away. He made the decision to go, and encouraged William to join him to hear what the preacher had to say. It was a great sermon and William was so interested and taken with the message from the book of Romans that he went again the next Sunday. It took nearly three hours to walk there and back but worth every forward footstep to faith. It was a small journey to a big destination. The sermon was based on Romans 3:25-26:

> God presented Christ as a sacrifice of atonement, through the shedding of His blood, to be received by faith. He did this to demonstrate His righteousness, because in His forbearance, He had left the sins committed beforehand unpunished, He did it to demonstrate His righteousness at the present time, so as to be just and the One who justifies those who have faith in Jesus.

This was the real Christian message in a nutshell. William realised that God had sent His Son to die for his sins. He had faith in Jesus and because of that he was justified and acceptable to God. William had not heard the message of the Gospel in this way before; it was different to anything he had experienced and it struck a chord deep inside of him. Jesus was the ultimate sacrifice and it was by grace that he was saved, and by no other means. There was nothing that he could do to achieve salvation and righteousness. Jesus had already done it. He shed His blood on the cross and died to make a way for everyone to be able to reconnect with God. It was by faith alone. It was a complete revelation to William and Robert.

From that day on William was desperate to be fed by the Word of God. His hunger for physical things diminished, whilst his spiritual hunger increased. He wanted to hear about this grace of God from anyone who would speak about it. He was drawn towards the place he had initially heard the message and it soon became a weekly walk to Thame to hear the fullness of the Gospel.

Then after years of searching, his personal life-changing miracle happened. He came into the light and the truth set him free. William at last understood the gift that Christ offered. He repented and asked forgiveness for his sins; accepting the grace and liberty that Christ had freely given him. He was born again. The chains of self-condemnation were broken and the course of his life was inevitably changed.

This conversion experience had the unexpected result of creating a time of loneliness and alienation in young William's life. Apart from his family, there was no one that understood the transformation in him. Long Crendon was not a God-fearing village; nearly everyone had a distaste for Christianity and its practices. It was described by a visiting stranger as a 'vile strangling place.' It was home to a history of darkness, shadows and secrets. The parish church was neglected both spiritually and physically and had been for many years. Its towering presence was a façade and played a very elementary role in the spiritual life of the villagers. There was no permanent vicar and its traditions were barely tolerated by both clergy and parishioners alike; it was a place for hatches, matches and dispatches and not much more.

People had difficult lives and Sundays were their only time off. The day was seen as a time for games, sports and drinking and more drinking into the night. Most inhabitants had no time for faith or religion in any form. An occasional preacher would make their way to the village to spread the good news but they were never welcomed.

On one such occasion, a well-meaning man from another settlement, walked to Long Crendon with the intention of preaching the Gospel. He placed himself under a big elm tree in the village square and began his message. Sadly, it was not well received. It ended abruptly when one of the villagers filled a water squirt with animal blood and shot it all over the preacher's face. He made a quick, embarrassed exit, leaving the heckles and laughter of the locals behind him.

The incident of the blood would not have gone unnoticed by William, but despite the state of the village, his faith in Christ gave him a zeal for the things of God; it was not something he wanted to hide. He was full of joy but also naïve as he pursued his search for deeper truths. William became unpopular overnight when it became common knowledge that he was attending Dissenter meetings in Thame. He was looked on with suspicion by both the church and the locals and it made him the object of many sneers, comments and foul language.

As he walked through the village on his way to attend a Gospel meeting, he would be jeered at and called a 'speckled bird' by his neighbours; a particular insult meaning that he did not fit in with them anymore. He was different to them and no longer welcome to be part of their community because of his faith. It was a hard lesson for a young man to learn. By becoming acceptable in God's eyes William had become unacceptable to the people of his home village.

William was hurt by the outbursts from former friends and neighbours but he did not let the jibes and rejection deter him. He continued following his own path, committed to God's way. Although, for his own self-preservation, whenever he was going to hear a sermon, he sensibly went the long way round, going two miles out of his way past Notley Mill. This way he did not have to walk through the high street, avoiding prying eyes and any inevitable confrontations.

It was into this climate of bullying and ostracisation that William and Mary's first child was brought into the world; a beautiful daughter called Sarah, bringing with her more joy, more love and the responsibility of another mouth to feed.

It was the spring of 1798. George the third had been on the throne for the last thirty-eight years and England was facing an ever-increasing threat of a French invasion. It was a time of worry for rich and poor alike; the future was uncertain for everyone but particularly hard for those with little or no resources to help cushion them in a time of crisis.

Regardless of national concerns, day-to-day life, for the young family, marched on, much in the same way it always had. Once the upheaval and euphoria of being a new parent had worn off, William's life became a relatively mundane routine. The weeks and months rolled into one as he spent long hours applying himself to the occupation of mending, making and selling clothes. Since the village had shunned him, local custom had become sparse and sporadic, but undeterred, he had a notion to go further afield to get trade from elsewhere. There was only one drawback with this idea and that was transport - he did not have any.

To solve the problem, he acquired an old wooden handcart to carry his goods. It was a solution of a kind but it was tedious and arduous work pushing the rickety two-wheeled vehicle along rough tracks, particularly in inclement weather. The cart seemed to have a personality of its own, always wanting to go in the opposite direction to its master, making steering it from hamlet to village an art in itself. Nevertheless, he walked miles selling his wares, meeting new clients and drumming up business.

At the end of his long working day, his evenings were inevitably short, with a brief respite for supper before it was time to sleep and rest his weary body, ready for an early morning start the next day.

Sundays were special. They were set apart and on those days he took the opportunity to worship outside of the village and learn more about the God he was getting to know. William was meeting other men and women, young and old, who believed in Jesus and His message of redemption. Strong friendships were being formed, giving him moral support and making it easier for him to cope with the antagonism of his neighbours.

New Beginnings

By late 1799, when he was twenty-three and the world was on the cusp of a new century, William and two of his new-found friends, James Bruce and Edward Hanson, came to the collective realisation that Long Crendon needed God. To this end, they agreed to make time to meet in William's house, once a week, for prayer. They kept this new initiative private, away from prying eyes; it had to be this way, for now, because of the Godless state of the village. William was not the only one who had received verbal abuse for being different, his companions had also faced insults and comments and none of them wanted to risk anything that would put a stop to their precious prayer time.

The three young men had a genuine, heartfelt, desire to see the village of Long Crendon transformed by God. They knew the power of prayer and their secret weekly meeting continued for a few months until the spring of the next year. They were fervent and committed, laying down a spiritual foundation until it was ready to be built on. When the time was right, they invited Mr Thomas Howlett to come and join their little group. He was a wealthy, local farmer, who lived in Long Crendon but served as a deacon for the Baptist church at Waddesdon Hill, eight miles away. He was well versed in Scripture and it was their desire that he would come along to share his knowledge, to teach them and expand on the word of God.

At the same time, they realised it was time to open up their gathering to other people. Any reticence that had previously held them back was now gone. It was time to stand up and be counted as followers of Christ.

The meetings continued with Thomas bringing the message each week. Any initial trepidation, regarding the reaction of the locals soon dissipated as the news spread and people began to join them. Surprisingly, one of their first guests was the man who, two years before, had sprayed blood all over the visiting preacher. He came, heard the Gospel and exchanged animal blood for the redeeming blood of Christ. God was moving. Cold hearts were warming up.

Throughout this time of new beginnings and nurturing, Mary was expecting their second child and on the 9th July 1800, their first son, Joseph (my great great great grandfather) was born.

William and Mary's life together was expanding, spiritually and physically. Their home was only small and with their new baby, lively toddler and all the visitors that now attended their meeting each week, it was becoming a tight squeeze. Numbers increased so quickly that it was not long before it became impossible to host the gatherings in their house anymore. They now had the positive problem of looking around for bigger premises.

The solution came with an offer from a Mr Brangwin. He was a prominent Baptist who owned a farm at the West end of the village. His house was already licensed for worship and so it made perfect sense to move their group to his premises. It was now common knowledge in the community that there were Christians meeting regularly to pray and learn about the Bible. The locals, however, rather than throw insults, wanted to join in. More and more people became interested in hearing the word of God and their numbers continued to increase.

It was just over two years after that first secret prayer meeting and their prayers had been answered in a powerful way. The plan was to form a church but meanwhile it was now time to broadcast who they were and be completely open to the wider community. William and his friends decided to hold their first public Sunday service on January 4th 1801.

It was a cold winter's day as they prepared for the meeting in Mr Brangwin's barn but the weather did not discourage the congregation. They were keen and enthusiastic, turning up prepared to sit in a draughty, damp, outbuilding. The prospect of listening to the word of God and fanning the flames of their hearts was more desirable to them than staying at home, warming themselves by open fires. It was a day that would stay long in their memories as Thomas Howlett preached on Colossians 1:28:

> He is the one we proclaim, admonishing and teaching everyone with all wisdom, so that we may present everyone fully mature in Christ.

Young William sat listening intently to his older friend expound on the verse. It was a great word. *He is the one we proclaim.* Jesus Christ is the one we proclaim. Jesus Christ is the one we announce. Jesus Christ is the one we declare publicly and that is exactly what they were doing on that January day over two hundred and twenty years ago.

As he listened, William realised that for him to mature in Christ there was a need for admonishment, caution and warning. There was also a requirement for wise biblical teaching so that he could understand the Gospel and grow. Paul, the writer of Colossians was not content with converting people to Christ, he desired maturity and this was what was being preached. William was taking note.

Salvation was only the beginning of his walk with God, there was now a whole lot of growing up to be done.

Not long after the first service in the barn, William felt compelled to start a diary, never knowing that his words would start a legacy that continues to this day. He woke up on January the 27th 1801, took up his pen, dipped it in ink and wrote:

'I arose this morning and retired to my closet, and read and meditated a little on God's word and attempted to pray, but my corruptions were so strong that I could not express a word. I attended a prayer meeting in the evening where I, with others, tried again to pray and before I closed my eyes in sleep I viewed myself and my actions in the past day and past life and was satisfied that I neither had done one single action in all my life, neither could I do without the grace of God but what is defiled with sin. Although God accepts His own

work in Christ, yet there is enough in the Christian's prayer to cause great work for repentance.'

On this particular day, as William started reading and reflecting on God's word, a moment of revelation and conviction came to him. He knew about the grace of Christ but on this day, he recognised the monumental extent of sin's effect without the redeeming work of Christ. He personalised it and began to ponder on his own shortcomings and failures. His thoughts went deep, being humbled, to the point that he could not pray. Words failed him as he realised that without God's grace everything was corrupted by sin.

William spent the whole day working it through, concluding that repentance was the key and that without the amazing grace of God, everything in his life would count as nothing.

Thomas continued to preach regularly throughout the winter, either in his house or in the barn. It was only ever a temporary move to make room for the ever-growing congregation as they waited, in faith, for another more suitable building to become available. By the beginning of spring, a new venue had been offered. It was a large house, situated to the south of the village belonging to a Mr Benham Crook. In May, of the same year, it was licensed and opened for public religious worship but this time offering two Sunday services to accommodate everyone that now wanted to attend.

Meanwhile, Mary was pregnant again and, in due time, gave birth to a son, Henry. William's family was growing along with his obligations. He now had three children to feed on his income from tailoring, as well as all his commitments to growing God's family. Life was becoming more difficult; lack of money and resources were becoming a constant battle in his daily walk. Deprivation and poverty were rearing their mocking heads again as if they were taunting him in his belief that God would always provide.

William continued in the absolute conviction of his own salvation. One of his diary entries was only short but said so much about the spiritual principles that he aligned himself with.

'I thought this day what a comfortable thing it is to have a prospect of Heaven and Jesus our friend. Lord, reveal these things more clearly to me.'

He was looking beyond the momentary things of the world and placing his faith in the permanent promises of Heaven. He had a close bond with Jesus and counted Him as a friend. This was not a formal relationship based on rules, regulations and fear. It was a close and personal connection with the son of God. He found comfort and security in thinking upon such things and wanted to understand more, praying that God would give him clear revelations of His truth.

William was now at a point in his spiritual walk when he wanted to be baptised. Unlike his childhood christening, it was a public declaration of his personal faith. It was to be a full immersion baptism, symbolically washing away his sins and identifying with the death and resurrection of Jesus.

This was a momentous occasion in William's life, one of those days whose date you never forget. It was the next step on his Christian path and an example of faith and obedience to all the people who came to witness the event and to all his neighbours who heard it on the village grapevine.

There was no baptistery in Long Crendon because adult baptism had never been practised in the village and so he was to be baptised elsewhere, in one of the local chapels that had the right facilities.

Baptism was a chance for William to publically declare his personal faith in Jesus. He wanted everyone to know that he had given his life to Christ and was prepared to spend the rest of his years following Him. It was to be a symbolic act identifying with the death, burial and resurrection of Jesus Christ.

There was a momentary hush in the chapel as William stood solemnly waiting at the side of the baptismal pool. The church congregation plus William's friends and family watched on as he, ceremonially and gingerly, made his way down the steps into the chilly water. The minister was waiting for him. For the second time in his life, the words I baptise you in the name of the Father the Son and the Holy Spirit, were said over him as he was lowered under the water, three times before finally being lifted up, leaving the old behind and raised up to a new life in Christ.

Mr Crook's house became the permanent home for meetings and on the 15th March 1802, the Baptist Church of Long Crendon was officially established with ten permanent members. Several members of Waddesdon Hill Baptist had been released to form the core of the church, under the leadership of Thomas Howlett.

The event started with a formal service where William was invited to stand up and read a statement of the 'leading of providence from the commencement until that day.' He was not used to taking centre stage but was happy to put his new skills to use. It was important for the congregation to know that from the small beginnings of those hidden prayer meetings, bountiful provision had been made both physically and spiritually, in order for the church to be established. The change in attitudes of the locals was nothing short of a miracle and William was determined to make sure that the gratitude and credit for all of it was given to God.

William had been an integral part of the church since its inception, and as such, he was a natural choice to be nominated as a deacon to serve the church with any practical need that may arise. A vote was taken by the holding up of hands and he was unanimously elected to the post. This was such a sign of respect and trust; the leaders were serious men of God and the decision to make William a deacon was not taken lightly. It was based on 1 Timothy 3:8-10 and 12:

> In the same way, deacons are to be worthy of respect, sincere, not indulging in much wine, and not pursuing dishonest gain. They must keep hold of the deep truths of the faith with a clear conscience. They must first be tested; and then if there is nothing against them, let them serve as deacons.

> A deacon must be faithful to his wife and must manage his children and his household well.

As a deacon, William had to be seen to be sincere, honest, sober, faithful and worthy of respect while taking good care of his family. He had to keep hold of the deep truths of the faith with a clear conscience. In other words, he had to walk the talk with his behaviour aligning up with his beliefs. The leaders had looked into William's life and character and not found him wanting.

The occasion was a momentous, happy one for everyone involved, with the celebrations going on for the whole day. The women of the congregation brought special food that they had been busy baking and preparing, creating a wonderful shared lunch for all to enjoy.

In the afternoon, the pews were once again filled as a sermon was preached on Acts 11:23:

> When he arrived and saw what the grace of God had done, he was glad and encouraged them all to remain true to the Lord with all their hearts.

There was a theme going on in William's life, and grace was the central message again. Previous to this verse in Acts, many people had believed and turned to the Lord because of God's grace. Grace is a powerful, transforming force in the process of conversion. People are brought into the light and souls are saved because of the love and favour of our Heavenly Father.

This was what the church in Long Crendon was all about. They wanted to see people come to Jesus and when it happened, they were glad and wanted to support them so that they could stay true to God with all their hearts. This was William's desire, to see salvation and regeneration come into the hearts of the men and women of his home village.

This day marked for William what would be the beginning, of a lifetime of dedication to God and service to others. He had a servant heart and as a deacon had to be practical to keep the church functioning at its best. He also knew that he wanted to be able to share the word and spread the Gospel. His yearning to preach filled him with passion but he was uneducated and found any type of speaking in public difficult. If he was going to fulfil the dream that God had placed on his heart, then it was going to prove a hard and demanding road to travel.

He was a young family man, from a small community who had lived in poverty all his life and had no preparation or training for any type of public work. However, despite all the obstacles, his longing to become a preacher was greater and he was determined to overcome all the limitations that had been placed on his life from birth.

He knew older men in the church that were themselves gifted and practised in the art of preaching, who would give him guidance and encouragement, but if he was to be successful then self-education was, again, his only option. He had taught himself to read and write and this fuelled his natural optimism in his ability to become more educated. With enthusiasm and regardless of his lack of free time, lack of money for books and no one to teach him, he began to learn. He spent time reading the Word, learning some Latin and Greek as he went along.

William also started studying Hebrew. If there was a rumour of a Jew in the village, he went out of his way to find them, even stopping them in the street. Bible in hand, he quizzed the stranger until his questions were resolved. In this way, he acquired the correct pronunciation and meaning of the language, going ever deeper into the meaning of different Bible passages. William was persistent and determined and even though it was difficult and demanding, he never relinquished his dream.

It was laborious and repetitive but God was with him and over time, he achieved his first major goal. He became proficient in understanding the original language of the Old Testament. The depth and breadth of his knowledge of Scripture was growing but it was not just head knowledge, his heart was keeping pace too as his love for God and others increased and matured.

William was now well versed but he had another obstacle to overcome. Although he now had the words in his head, the art of actually voicing them out to other people was a completely different ability. Without the self-confidence and poise that a good education and wealth can often give, preaching did not come naturally to him. It was challenging but he had already proved that he was not a man to be beaten and so he began to practice the art of speaking out.

William's first attempts were in private, when no one was listening as he stumbled, stuttered and made mistakes. Each time he spoke out, he became a little more self-assured. Before long he was practising on friends and family, knowing that in their company he was safe from non-constructive criticism. It was a big leap but, eventually, the day came when he had enough courage and ability to undertake his first sermon in front of a congregation.

As he stepped up to the pulpit, he drew his strength from God as he voiced out personally revealed spiritual truths. God had given him the desires of his heart. As he spoke, his words were well received and before long, William attained a degree of respectability as a public speaker. One of the notable points about William's sermons was his lack of prepared notes; he spoke directly from the heart, relying on the Holy Spirit to prompt and direct him. The young man who a few years before could not even read, had come a long way.

Growing

William was growing in character and maturing in spirit. He was digging deep into the word, and the truth was regularly being revealed to him. After one significant day of reflection, he sat down and wrote:

'I saw this evening that nothing could give me any satisfaction in this world; my mind seemed weaned from all earthly objects; I could delight but in one thing – to be doing something for Jesus Christ.'

William had a selfless nature; his desire was to labour for Jesus; to speak His name and make Him known to others. Despite his lack of material possessions, he had no interest in worldly things. Even at a young age, he knew that the indulgences and recreational diversions of life were temporary distractions. His focus was on Jesus Christ.

This is not to say that the demands of everyday living did not affect William. Of course they did. He was human with all the frailties and failings that are part and parcel of our earthly minds and bodies. Throughout his life, he had already suffered a lot of deprivation and hardship and often had to go without but his physical sufferings always produced a faith-generated response.

'Very much distressed for temporal things this day. No money. Oh what trials! Yet I experience that the Lord gives me strength equal to the day.'

Pity parties were not even a contemplation for William. He acknowledged his need and lack of material possessions, but never blamed God. His experience was that God's power saw him through. A measure of strength, physical and spiritual would be given to him daily to balance out whatever life had to throw at him.

One of his diary entries was as follows:

'A very dark prospect this day indeed; but still I was enabled to trust in God and He did provide bountifully, and I was enabled to see that He does all things well; insomuch, that I thought if I were to live my time over again, I would not be without the troubles I have had and am likely to have, and from which I can see no way of escape.'

William trusted God for everything, even in his darkest days. It was a deep, *resting in Him* confidence, always grateful for His Father's bounties, no matter how small. He did not expect his troubles to be taken away; he saw them as temporary and unimportant within his spiritual perspective. He fixed his eyes on Jesus and on the things of eternity.

'Such a day as this I never experienced before. In the morning was very cold and flat in frame, and had only some parsnips and a little bit of bread for dinner. About two o'clock, I set off for Chearsley, where I expected to take some money. I thought, as I went along, how kind the Lord was to us in sending such a prospect of wheat etc. and how rebellious we are against Him, and how unkind to each other. When I got to Chearsley, I was disappointed in taking my money and returned with my mind full of anxiety, for I expected the people would say something about the money; so I went on so full, that I thought I should burst. I prayed to the Lord to help, and give me strength, and my mind grew more composed; still, like Habakkuk, trusting in a faithful God, I thought how glad I should be if the Lord would send me something to eat. When I got home I was faint and weary from want, and I found that by the special providence of God my sister had sent a barley cake, which was so acceptable and so sweet that I ate it with much satisfaction; and I saw clearly that the Lord was not confined to the means I had made use of. Blessed be the name of the Lord.'

William's diligent perseverance was never for financial gain but always for spiritual advancement of himself and others. In this diary extract he had walked to the village of Chearsley, a five mile round trip, with little food in his stomach, expecting to be paid for some work that he had done. It seems that no talk of payment ever happened and he could not, or would not, ask for recompense, so he came back without any money. Instead of blaming God for the situation he found himself in, he prayed and asked Him for strength.

It seems his prayers were answered by the provision of a barley cake from his younger sister, Annie. It was more of a sweet loaf than a cake, made with barley grain, which was so much cheaper than wheat and a common bread substitution for the poor. For William, the gift was like manna from Heaven, at a time when he was faint from hunger. Within this, he acknowledged the fact that God's ways are not our ways and to expect the unexpected if we trust in Him.

William and Mary remained poor all their lives. They never gained any worldly wealth but received so many more blessings of a more permanent nature.

In 1803, another son, John, made his appearance into their busy household. William, now twenty-seven and Mary twenty-nine, with four children under the age of five, made for a lot of challenges and opportunities.

The church continued to meet in Mr Crook's house until, after a couple of years, it had grown both financially and numerically, enabling them to start making plans to build their first bespoke church building. The site they were able to purchase was down Frogmore lane, a dark, narrow, meandering track to the west of the village. The site was cheap and had its drawbacks. It was situated half way down a hill and, therefore, the land was often marshy and water logged. The work began in earnest with everyone pitching in, according to their abilities. The men laboured, in their spare time, while the women provided food, drink and encouragement for the workers.

It was a basic building, without pomp or ornamentation, a place to worship God. By 1806, all the hard work had come to fruition. The inside of the chapel was swept and cleaned and the pews polished until their wood shone in anticipation of welcome guests. It was finally ready for use, along with its very own baptistery! It was only small but it was purpose built and now the church had a real presence in the village.

The building of the new church was very timely for the local inhabitants. Long Crendon, like the rest of the country, had been suffering from the effects of the Napoleonic wars for the past few years. The army and navy had been on high alert and enlistment of soldiers and volunteers had been heavily encouraged. Defences, particularly in the south of the country, had been reinforced and new ones built, all at extra cost to the parishioners.

Taxes had been introduced for all, apart from the poorest in society, in an effort to fund the war. Trade restrictions caused unemployment and food prices had soared, leaving people unable to provide for themselves or their families. Many men and women were left in abject misery, teetering on the brink of starvation. The scarcity of food and money drove husbands, sons and brothers to enlist in the army; at least they were getting paid. Married men were discouraged from joining with the fear that they would be leaving their families to starve but many felt they had little choice; their loved ones were already weak and sick with hunger. This often left their wives and children to the mercy of the parish.

People were in need and the economic backdrop of the country acted as an unexpected catalyst for the little chapel down Frogmore Lane. The locals began to consider their spiritual standing and turned to this new place of worship for guidance. With Jesus at its centre and committed Christians willing to help, the church began to have an impact on the Godless community. Lives were transformed. Christ's light was penetrating the darkness; shifting the soulless shadows that had held the neighbourhood in chains for far too many decades.

It was also a season for a very bad outbreak of an alarming disease called *jail fever* (endemic typhus) within the locality. The outbreak had been brought in by a malnourished ex-prisoner who, on release from the local prison, had unwittingly carried the disease back to Crendon. He had come from an overcrowded, filthy, cold, deprived septic place and he was filthy, without any opportunity to wash for months. He smelt like a sewer. Hundreds of lice had made their home on his body and hair. He was itching and scratching all day; irritated by the little red bite marks from scores of lice. It was common to be bitten by tiny insects whilst stagnating next to dozens of other prisoners, and so he thought little about it, totally unaware that he was already sick. The lice were infected and *jail fever* was now silently swimming in his blood, invading his body and growing in strength.

He reached Long Crendon and spent time renewing old acquaintances; begging former friends for bread, unaware of the deadly disease inside him, biding its time. Unfortunately, before the poor, broken man exhibited any symptoms he had been in contact with lots of people. Fresh blood was on the agenda and the lice had taken their opportunity to jump onto other unsuspecting victims. A circle of cruel contagion had begun.

A week went by before throbbing pain began pulsing through his head. The infection had taken hold. He felt hot and drowsy as fatigue overwhelmed him. The fever fanned its flames until his skin radiated out the fiery furnace within. He could hardly move as nausea rose from the pit of his stomach, followed by retching and vomiting until his body was spent and he was still. He lay there; agonizing pain his only companion.

He had longed for freedom but now he was a prisoner again, imprisoned by a sickness that constrained him in a dark place that reeked of death. He stayed in this state for a few days until a rash appeared as the toxins invaded his whole body. There was no treatment for this wretched man; there was only one way this was going to end. Gangrene began to develop; turning his flesh a green tinted black as his flesh dried up and rotted away. His breathing became laboured as pneumonia developed, attacking and inflaming his lungs. It was time to sleep. He shut his eyes for the last time and silently slipped into a coma; a blessed release before his death.

By now, it was common knowledge that 'jail fever' had entered the village and fear settled like a shroud over their little community. The lice had done their job well and before long the next person, and the next person and the next person, suffered the same horrific fate. William watched and prayed as death took its toll. He wrote:

'Many persons of all ages were swept into the grave, to the great dismay of the survivors.'

For many, this human tragedy gave rise to a spiritual awakening. Folks were frightened and more men, women and children started to look beyond themselves for safety and security. In their hour of need, they turned to God.

Frogmore Lane church became a place of sanctuary for the scared, the grieving and the lost.

The small meeting house was filled on the Lord's Day, many attended the weekly prayer meeting, and from this time the dissenting interest increased.'

It was a time of renewal in hearts that had grown cold and a time of fresh faith and fellowship.

William remained in his post as a deacon for the next seven years reaching out to others on a practical and spiritual level. There was much building-up to be done. The men and women of the church were the hands and feet of Jesus, working at the front line of a village steeped in poverty and pain. William was part of the team nurturing the growing congregation as he served and occasionally preached in the village and its outlying areas.

As well as the responsibilities at church, William maintained a conscientious work and home life. He had established himself as the main village tailor, working hard for his family. All the garments were made by hand, with a skill that had been perfected over the years. Mary was always there, cleaning, cooking, looking after the children, lace making and supporting William. Together they served their God, united in His love. In 1810, Mary gave birth to Ann; a sister to Sarah, 12; Joseph, 10; Henry, 9 and seven-year-old John.

William's preaching started to be noticed. He became known as the man who preached without notes; someone whose heart was in the words that came out of his mouth. His sermons were less stuffy and formulaic than they would have been had he written his sermon out the week before and just read it out verbatim. The congregation liked this fresh approach and his popularity as a speaker grew. It was a far cry from his early nervous days of public speaking.

News travelled and he was sought out to preach in churches further afield. On a Sunday in March 1811, when he was thirty-five, William was invited to preach at the Particular Baptist Church at Aylesbury, eleven miles away. He accepted the invitation, and his sermon was well received. He continued to go and preach at irregular intervals, speaking the words that God had given him in maturity and truth. The leaders and the congregation were much taken by him and two years on from his first visit, they asked him if he would consider being their minister.

Many of the churches in Buckinghamshire at that time were Particular Baptists, including Long Crendon. Their views were Calvinistic and as such, they believed that only a predestined elect would be saved. Although William's Christian journey started with these views (many of the men who he looked up to were Calvinistic,) as he got older he sought the truth for himself and his beliefs on this matter mellowed.

To take up or decline the position at Aylesbury was a difficult decision. If he accepted the job, then it meant leaving the fellowship at Long Crendon, a place that had become his spiritual home, and an integral part of his life, since its commencement. He spent much time in prayer, to see if it was a God idea and not just a good idea. Eventually, after seeking guidance he believed that God confirmed that this was the right direction for him. He accepted the position at Aylesbury and relinquished his role as deacon, officially leaving with the blessings of his minister, friends and family. He knew that it was going to be a challenge, with trials along the way but he faced it with his usual fortitude and embraced the opportunity with praying hands.

Minister in the Making

William was publicly ordained at Aylesbury on Thursday July 29th 1813. It was a very solemn occasion, attended by Baptist leaders from all over the region, including London, many of them taking an active part in the ordination ceremony.

He sat there surrounded by all those that knew and respected him, grateful for God's bountiful blessings in his life. The service started with Scripture readings and prayer, followed by a statement on the reasons for dissent from the established church. The proceedings continued, as William addressed the congregation, to give his confession of faith; a statement of his belief and doctrine. The ordination prayer finalised the formalities as William was officially set apart in his new role as a minister of the church.

The service continued and Mr Shenstone of London delivered the charge to William from 1 Timothy 6:20-21:

> Timothy, guard what has been entrusted to your care. Turn away from godless chatter and the opposing ideas of what is falsely called knowledge, which some have professed and in so doing have departed from the faith. Grace be with you all.

In the first part of these verses, William was encouraged and empowered to guard the Gospel that God had put in his care. He was charged to protect the pulpit and the truth of the Bible. He knew the authenticity of Scripture and was entreated to preach with integrity, without watering down the message. The second half of the reading was an instruction to beware of distractions. He was to avoid empty worldly talk and not to entertain false knowledge that claimed to be more reliable than God's word. His challenge was to be resolute and steadfast in his belief and proclamations of truth.

This message was a blueprint for the rest of William's ministry as he endeavoured to be a faithful servant for Christ, walking the old fashioned narrow path; keeping his focus on the things of God. In his own words William believed that *'the Scriptures addressed man as a rational and responsible creature, at the same time asserting the purpose of God to stain his pride and humble his haughty looks.'*

After the specific exhortation for William, came a longer sermon directed to the congregation. Mr. Seymour had come from Great Missenden, sixteen miles away to preach on 1 Thessalonians 3:8:

> For now we really live, since you are standing firm in the Lord.

This verse was written by the apostle Paul in a letter that he sent to the church in Thessalonica in Macedonia. Paul had spent a few weeks in Thessalonica along with his companion Silas. While they were there, they visited the town's synagogue for three Sabbaths in a row, taking time to explain the prophesies in Scripture to prove that Christ was the Jews' long awaited Messiah. Some of the men and women who heard Paul's words were convinced and joined them, including Jews, Gentiles and Romans, each one of them finding a new freedom in Christ.

Others, however, were jealous and gathered up local troublemakers to create a riot. The situation became dangerous and untenable so, in order to protect Paul and Silas, the believers sent them quietly out of Thessalonica. They travelled to a small town about fifty miles away.

Out of necessity, Paul had to leave this small band of new believers, young in faith but strong in spirit, to manage on their own. Consequently, he was worried about them because he knew they were under persecution from their own countrymen. They were suffering for their faith and although Paul was desperate to be with them, it was difficult and risky for him to return to

Thessalonica. Instead he sent Timothy to them to give them strength and encouragement so that they would know they were not alone.

After a while, Timothy returned to Paul with a positive report about the believers he had spent time with. Despite all their troubles, they were remaining strong in their faith. Paul was relieved to learn that the Thessalonians were standing firm and remaining resilient through hard times. In response, he penned a letter to them, including the words for now we really live, since you are standing firm in the Lord.

As William listened to the sermon, he knew the relevancy of the message for him and his fellow believers. For many years, they had struggled against the anti-Dissenter stance of the state church. They battled for the freedom to worship and serve God; suffering personal and corporate discrimination, intimidation and harassment. Even at this point, there were cases where state clergymen refused to bury the corpses of Dissenters, when there were no alternatives available, even though the law stated that they should unless the individual in question had not been christened as a child. The law would be enforced eventually but it caused a great deal of emotional turmoil and practical issues when there was such lack of cooperation from the parish church. The rejection did not stop there. It reached its petty hands out to the community, into shops that took delight in snubbing Dissenter customers, so they had to go elsewhere for their bread and other products.

Not to be outdone, the believers set up their own bakery and other shops to service the Baptists, the Wesleyans and any other Nonconformists that passed through. One of their members owned a grocer shop and decided to diversify to help his fellow Baptists. He put an advert into the local paper stating that he was 'appoint agent to the protestant Dissenters and general life and fire assurance company,' hoping that it would be of essential interest to the dissenting community. Sadly, it was very much a case of 'us and them' as William and his flock were seen as trouble makers, because they refused to conform to the constraints of the state church.

The discriminations and intimidations were real enough, affecting the minds and lives of those living in Long Crendon, but not to the dreadful depths of those that had come before. There was a long history in Buckinghamshire of men being persecuted for their principles; branded with hot irons, charged with heresy because they stood firm, and burnt at the stake for their beliefs. Over the centuries, many men and women of God had walked the path and lit the way. Now it was William's turn to walk in their footsteps, to follow a road that they had prepared. He was treading on the very ground where lives had been sacrificed for their faith.

One hundred and fifty years before his time, it had been illegal for more than five adults to group together for Nonconformist worship. If they did and were caught, then a fine, imprisonment or even transportation was deemed suitable retribution. Despite all the opposition, or maybe because of it, small clusters of Christ's followers began to shoot up. Initially it was all kept very quiet but the groups soon became organised. There was strength in unified numbers and non-conformity began to find its voice.

Out of this, many sects appeared, including the Anabaptists - the forerunners of the Baptist church. The fight became political, it had to and after several hard fought campaigns, there was a major breakthrough. By 1689, the Toleration Act was passed, granting restrictive freedom of worship for all non-conformists. The struggle for freedom from religious man-made restraints had been a long battle but it was a battle worth fighting for, and in some cases, dying for.

This new Act at the end of the 17th century encouraged a few people to start up a Nonconformist church in Long Crendon. It began with enthusiasm, and without fear, because they could now meet for worship without reprisal. Sadly, it only ever served a few faithful and by 1726, it had closed its doors.

Change takes time and although their services were legal, they were still met with much opposition from unofficial sources. General religious apathy was sweeping across the country leaving the village in the hands of the irrelevant, neglected, parish church for seventy-five years. The village became a dark, hard place, with very little evidence of God-fearing folk. That is, until William and his friends had begun to pray.

This was the history that William inherited. A trail blazed for hundreds of years whose fire had never been fully extinguished. He had the freedom to worship in ways that his predecessors had not but socially and politically Nonconformists were still seen as second-class citizens. There was opposition, disapproval and obstruction from many sides. He was not in danger of being burnt at the stake, nevertheless he was being called to stand strong in the Lord and William was a man of his word.

Aylesbury Baptist Church congregation were blessed to have William as their minister for several years. He was an industrious and reliable leader, preaching the Good News and tending to his flock. It was a new and exciting time: a season of growth where he was always willing to go the extra mile. His work was a vocation, not a duty or a means to a financial end. He gave willingly of himself to others, for the betterment of their lives.

The Buckinghamshire area was still shrouded in a light veil of contempt and disrespect when it came to alternative forms of religion. In 1815, there was an incident that was worthy of a mention in the national Baptist Magazine. Its dramatic heading read 'Riots at The Baptist Meeting House, Longwick, Bucks.'

On a winter's Sunday evening, the congregation were assembling for worship when they were 'repeatedly alarmed by bricks and stones thrown against the windows and door and by external and tumultuous shouts and clamour.'

One of the men went outside and managed to apprehend the main offender who was subsequently prosecuted by the Committee of the Protestant Society at the suggestion of Lord Carrington who was a neighbouring magistrate. The delinquent, with the help of some influential friends, had tried his best to delay the trial and punishment. However, the law caught up with him and the Society indicted him under a new Act for disturbing the congregation.

After his trial, which lasted many hours, he was found guilty as charged. Unfortunately, for him, this new act had doubled the former penalty for such behaviour with no leeway for the judge to be lenient. He was sentenced to pay the sum of £40.

Things were beginning to look up for Nonconformists. They were no longer being overlooked, with acts being passed to help safeguard them from persecution. The comment from the end of the trial by the prosecutors summed up the beginnings of change:

'We regret the necessity for such proceedings; but as they are unfortunately too frequently required we are happy that a Society exists, which without any respect to parties, or to denominations, affords protection and security to all Dissenters who need their interposition and assistance.'

The political climate concerning freedom of religion was shifting but it would take several years for the attitudes to filter down into daily life. The experience of a Baptist minister was still going to be fraught with tests and trials. William was committed to God's cause and was very tenacious and steadfast in his approach to work. If an obstacle was put in his way, he would devise a plan to get around it or over it; whatever was required for the greater good.

During his tenure at Aylesbury, their last three children, James, Elizabeth and William were born. Mary was forty-eight when she gratefully gave birth to her last child in 1822. Three years previously, their eldest daughter had tied the knot and left the nest. Even so, conditions in their home were more cramped than ever. They still lived in their small High Street house with nine offspring, whose ages ranged from newborn to twenty-two. There was no privacy for any of them. It was a busy time for William; he now had to walk a sixteen-mile round trip every time he was required at chapel.

Meanwhile, the Baptist church in Long Crendon had, at first, continued to grow steadily with Thomas Howlett at the helm. Unfortunately, not long after William had moved on, Thomas' health began to decline. He was suffering from a painful and lingering illness that laid him very low, to the point that he could only preach occasionally. He passed away at the age of sixty-one having served faithfully since a young man. He had been a cultured and educated man, with good social skills, whose conduct and character had always been exemplary.

Thomas had always had a generous heart and even in death, his benevolent nature shone through as he bequeathed a good sum of money to two Christian societies, also leaving £200 to the Crendon church to support the next minister. Unfortunately, this last bequest became void because he had written it into his will within a year of his death. Nevertheless, his dying wishes had been to support the work of the Kingdom in his home church.

Thomas had been a great friend, teacher and mentor to William over the years and his loss was felt deeply. His death was also a big blow to the sixty or so members of the congregation. He had shepherded them from the small beginnings of the church, keeping the place steady and secure with his plain talking sermons. He was going to be missed.

A search was now on for a new minister but there was no one locally who could oversee all the duties that Thomas had undertaken. Consequently, the church soon began to flounder; there was dissention and division within the congregation. They could not agree on a way forward and meetings were cancelled, even on Sundays. Spiritual foundations were being tested and the vision was beginning to fade.

This lack of unity could not have happened at a worse time. Life was exceptionally hard for many of the locals as the deprivation of the war years was leaving even more of its miserable mark. The ordinary men and women of the village had been plunged into deep poverty; there was very little food to go around with the poorest subsisting on black barley bread alone. Malnutrition was an unwelcome guest in many homes and some unfortunates turned to crime to help fill the bellies of their families. This was a risky business for if you were caught the punishments were harsh.

One young Crendon man, tried to steal two pecks of potatoes (about sixty potatoes) from a local farmer's barn, no doubt in order to feed his hungry family. He was caught, tried, found guilty and sentenced to three months in prison. This left him locked away in atrocious, life threatening conditions, with his family left to the mercy of the parish and their paltry outdoor relief. (A benefit for the homeless and destitute to make sure they did not starve).

Food, and how to get it, was a top priority for those without. Hunger drove one man to be tempted by two bushels of peas (about forty pounds in weight). He was imprisoned to do hard labour for a year. One soon to be prisoner, broke into a house and stole a loaf of bread, four pounds of bacon and other unnamed articles and was sentenced to fourteen year's transportation. Two thieves, working together, broke into two local houses, taking various items and for this, they both received the death penalty.

Not everyone that was poor turned to crime, the majority of people remained law abiding citizens, almost passively accepting their lot in life, trying to get through by begging, borrowing or benefiting from the occasional charitable donation. The wealthy landowners did at times show benevolence; reducing tithes when agricultural output was low and distributing goods to the needy at various times of the year. However, it was impossible for them to comprehend what it was like to live in poverty.

In the winter of 1825, the Oxford University and City Herald printed the following article:

> 'On Thursday last was distributed to the industrious and deserving poor of Long Crendon, twelve pair of Witney blankets, in addition to seventy-two pair, which were distributed the two preceding years, making a total of 84 pair, the gift of Lord and Lady Churchill; so that 119 families, 28 widows and 21 old, sick and infirm persons have received a blanket from their bountiful hands, for which the receivers desire to offer their best thanks, begging for the blessing of the Almighty to rest upon those hands which have been so liberally stretched out towards them and that such goodness might be rewarded a hundred-fold.'

I am sure the *deserving poor* were grateful for the added warmth to get them through a harsh winter but the struggle to survive was their reality, with starvation, for some, an ever present threat. Legal solutions were hard to come by; in a society based upon class, the poor did not have a voice. This left people desperate for practical and moral support.

Fortunately, the declining Baptist church still had a core of *faithfuls* whose eyes were open to the need around them. They held a meeting and decided they would keep the Sabbath School running in order to serve the local community. It was a beacon of light for struggling families. The parents were grateful for a much needed break and it gave the children a few hours of something positive in their young lives. Most of the youngsters had never been to any type of school and this afforded them the opportunity to learn to read and write.

Biblical teaching was also high on the agenda as they sat and listened about a man called Jesus who was the Saviour of the world. For some it was just a way to pass the time. For others, a seed would put its roots down and grow into maturity as they journeyed through life.

Attendance began to grow and, over time, as more parents put their trust in them, they began to reach more of the population. Despite the deprivation and disease in the community, the practical and spiritual needs of the young were being fed and nurtured.

The small membership of the church continued serving, despite the changes and challenges that came their way. They were devoted, dedicated and dependable, waiting patiently until a new minister was found in the form of a Rev. Spring, who arrived and took over the ministerial duties immediately. He turned out to be a man of great character, loved by the inhabitants for both his conduct and preaching. The church opened up again for Sunday and mid-week meetings. A sense of order reigned again. However, for personal reasons, his time at the church was short lived, being soon replaced by Rev. Williams.

This new minister was also popular but he did not stay for long and within months, the church was again left rudderless, drifting without leadership.

William was still living and working in the village as well as running the church in Aylesbury but he seemed an obvious solution to this dilemma. The members knew and trusted William and so approached him, asking if he would consider taking up pastoral charge at his home church.

It was another big decision. He did not answer straight away. There was much to consider and, as was his practice, William spent time praying and deliberating about the matter. He had been at his first ministerial post for seven years, putting down roots, creating relationships and growing alongside his flock. He wanted to make the right choice.

After much pondering and weighing up, an outcome was reached. He gave notice at Aylesbury. He walked the three-hour journey for one last time, preaching his final sermon to a congregation who had welcomed him in and were now sad to see him go. God wanted him back at the church that had been on his heart since he was a young man, where he had served faithfully as a deacon, but this time he was to be their minister. He was a founder member, his prayers and praise part of the fabric of the place. The wefts and warps of God's tapestry were being beautifully weaved.

Home is Where the Heart is

William's acceptance to be minister was made twenty-three years after he had first heard the call, to pray for his village. So much had happened before and during that time. He had gone from an uneducated, illiterate boy, to a respected teacher and *proclaimer* of God's word. He had gone from a young man desperate to be able to provide for his mother, to an experienced tailor able to support a large family of his own. He had gone from a lost child, without a dad to guide him, to a son of a Heavenly Father whose grace had given him a plan and purpose for his life.

On the 29th May 1822, at the age of forty-six, William was publicly recognised as the pastor of Long Crendon Baptist Church. He had come home. The ceremony commenced, Scriptures were read and prayers were spoken. The leading principles of dissent were stated and William was asked to profess his faith and belief in Jesus Christ, a belief that had never wavered and one in which he had always stood strong.

Mr Williams, a visiting minister, offered the ordination prayer and addressed the new pastor from 1 Timothy 6:11:

> But you, man of God, flee from all this, and pursue righteousness, godliness, faith, love, endurance and gentleness.

William, like Timothy, was being acknowledged as a man of God. He knew the Scriptures and was aware of what he was being asked to run from. The previous verse says:

> For the love of money is a root of all kinds of evil. Some people, eager for money, have wandered from the faith and pierced themselves with many griefs.

This was the charge given to William as he took his position as minister with an instruction to run from the desire for wealth and to pursue a Godly life. He was directed to pursue righteousness, to be holy of heart, to follow after faith, not to seek things seen but things unseen, not temporal but eternal matters. He was further directed to pursue love, the love of Christ and to embrace endurance in all things including persecution for the sake of the Gospel. Finally, he was charged to be gentle and humble and not to seek recognition.

This was a mighty challenge but one that he endeavoured to live up to for the rest of his life.

The celebrations went on for the whole day and in the afternoon, Mr Terry preached to the church from 1 Thessalonians 5:12-13:

> Now we ask you, brothers and sisters, to acknowledge those who work hard among you, who care for you in the Lord and who admonish you. Hold them in the highest regard in love because of their work. Live in peace with each other.

This was a timely and appropriate verse to give to a church that had just come out of a lean time of division and sporadic leadership. The final exhortation given to the Thessalonian church was used as a new beginning for the church of Long Crendon. It was an encouragement to give William and the other leaders the respect and support necessary to keep a committed body of believers united in their quest to be faithful and serve the Lord. There had been much discord and disagreement in the past but going forward the encouragement was for unity and harmony, to live in peace with one another. The scene was being set for William to play his part in God's plan.

The service concluded with these words from one of the leaders:

'Judging from the appearance of things on this interesting occasion we hope to see a great revival of zeal and practical piety.'

William and his flock were to be doers and not just speakers of the word. The village was in desperate need and this small band of men and women were to be co-labourers with Christ. They were being called to be His light in a place of brokenness, to preach the Gospel, to serve and to heal the hurt.

So began William's tenure as a minister in the village of his birth. Regular services were held as he preached from his pulpit, and his heart, speaking the truth and leading others to Christ.

Not satisfied with just reaching out locally, he wanted to spread the Gospel into outlying areas, and so began to extend out to other settlements. On Thursday nights, meetings were held in the village of Ickford, four miles south-west of Crendon. It started gently but William was committed and resolute and continued visiting every week until, after three years, the people were spiritually well-fed and prepared.

As a result, a small church sprang up, with men and women ready to pray and serve their community. The new venture had God's blessing on it. It soon progressed so well that their place of worship became too small to house the ever-growing congregation. In order to rectify the situation, a group of friends collectively raised funds to purchase a plot of land, with a plan to build a new church. The design was finalised and they set to, digging out foundations and building up walls. They had built up to about four feet and all was seemingly going well until hostility and conflict struck. Some of the locals did not want the Dissenters in their village and they had been waiting to make their move. One night, after all the workers had gone home, they entered the site and tore down the walls.

The Baptists were shocked and dismayed when they saw all their hard work in ruins but the whole episode made them even more resolute as they patiently began to rebuild. To avoid a repeat episode, they decided that from that moment on they would keep watch by day and night - and that is exactly what they did. The site was never left unattended, until it was completed. Such was their steadfastness and determination.

William also oversaw a Sabbath School and public worship that was facilitated at Oakly, another village to the north-west. More and more people were turning up each week to hear the central message about God's grace and the saving blood of Jesus Christ. The message was spreading. God's Spirit was moving; refreshing the souls of those who heard, received and responded.

The light of Jesus was now blazing, opening the eyes of the spiritually blind. Long Crendon and the surrounding area were experiencing the beginnings of revival. Church membership increased and a fresh wind blew through the dusty streets of the village. There was a hunger and passion for the things of God. Difficult days still lay ahead. People were still poor. Death and disease still destroyed lives but now there was faith, trust and hope: a hope in a saviour who offered them an eternity with Him.

William's home was situated right in the heart of the community. His days were demanding. He was in the habit of rising early to pray and spend time with the Lord before his time was swallowed up. He shared his hours between Mary and the children, tailoring, ministerial duties and caring for the congregation. His older offspring were, by now, young adults, getting married and expecting beautiful blessings of their own. Mary and William were going to be grandparents.

The church was going from strength to strength and in 1828, the meetinghouse in Frogmore was seen to be inconvenient. The church was in one of the worst positions in the village and in bad weather the land became very muddy and boggy, which proved to be quite a hindrance to the women in their boots and long dresses. Numbers were growing and it became obvious that another building would be advantageous.

Financially they had been provided for by some of the wealthier members of the congregation and so were able to start actively looking for new premises. They bided their time until an opportunity came along to buy and convert an old schoolroom that also had a small plot of land adjoining it. The site was close to the main thoroughfare of the village and in a much better situation. Before long, a small chapel was constructed, with room for more people, and a burial ground, although no baptistery was built. They kept the old meetinghouse so it could still be used for special occasions, including baptisms.

The new church had its grand opening on the 24th September 1829. It was an exciting time and acted as a catalyst for a rapid rise in the number of people in the congregation. By 1831 a widespread revival had occurred with over one hundred and fifty people attending on a regular basis and thirty-four young people being baptised, many of them young adults.

Fighting the Good Fight

The church attracted members from all walks of society but unusually a large number of them were quite affluent tradesmen and farmers, unlike other chapels who had smaller, more underprivileged congregations. Such was the generosity of these people that that the Baptist Church ended up in the unique position of having more money than the parish church. This was fabulous as they were able to reach out to those in need and offer much needed assistance. They could help feed those who were hungry and provide aid for the desperate and destitute. William had a heart for those in such dire situations; he remembered well his days of want and near starvation.

The financial security that the church found itself in was such a blessing from God but it was not appreciated by everyone. One of those people was a local vicar. The state church collected a tax known as the church rate. This was a common-law compulsory payment that parishioners had to pay. Payment received went towards the costs of the running services, repairs on the church building and the salaries of the clergy.

The Nonconformists, who paid for their own chapels, churches and ministers, on principle, did not think it was morally right for them to have to pay these taxes, as they did not use the facilities of the parish church. The state church also received funding from parliament while Nonconformist churches received nothing. This was a bone of contention in Long Crendon with some Baptists refusing to pay. This often came at a great cost. One respectable farmer, when at a Dissenter meeting, voted in the majority, against the compulsory church rate. As a consequence of this, he received notice from the landowner to quit his farm, after spending much time and labour bringing it into a proper state of cultivation. The persecution continued.

When the local vicar realised that the Dissenter chapel had more wealth than he did, despite his regular state payments, he was most affronted and so began a long running antagonism between the two parties.

The vicar was a man of mixed character. He cared about his parishioners and did a lot to help the impoverished and destitute. He was quite political on a local level, often speaking up for those in society that did not have a voice. He saw injustice and was not afraid to speak up to try and balance the scales. However, a lot of his focus was on money and he was not happy at all that the Baptist church was thriving. He was an anti-Dissenter, and bad feelings were aimed towards William and other Baptists.

He spent his time trying to discredit William and the Baptist church, along with other Nonconformists in the neighbourhood. As part of his campaign, he published a very long letter in the local newspaper. It was addressed to the inhabitants of Long Crendon. He called it *Voluntaryism* (That Curse on Good Government) Disproved from Scripture and Experience. The voluntaryism he was referring to was the principle of Dissenter churches and chapels supporting themselves with individual monetary contributions rather than with state funds. He had a problem with the fact that they were not state run and controlled. In his letter he didn't mince his words and referred to the Dissenters as *Men of corrupt minds, Prating puppies, Whimsical and obscure men, Virulent mob-courting republicans, Moon struck bigots with devilish and malignant motives, Poor deluded hearers, Wolves by nature, and Ministers of Satan with the curse of God resting upon them.*

He went on to directly attack William accusing him of being less than honest with the chapel's finances. Throughout, he was abusive and intolerant; a message broadcast from a man of the cloth with a big axe to grind.

The letter was set out in public domain, in the hope that everyone would see how heretical the Dissenters were and turn back towards the state church. William read it with dismay but remembered the verse he had been charged with all those years ago when he first became a minister – to guard what had been entrusted to him.

William replied, but not in the same attitude. He wrote a letter, of similar length and entitled it *The Voluntary Principle, the Religion of the Bible, and a Blessing in the World.*

On the first page, he wrote:

'The following address is designed to invite candid investigation, as truth, like gold, will bear to be tried'

He stated that everyone had a right to their opinions but within this people should be civil and courteous. He encouraged all Christians to understand the freedom that they had been given, the gifts they had received in terms of ministry and to understand that they were adopted into God's family. He also gave a very good discourse on the voluntary principle, urging people to seek their own salvation through Jesus and not to rely on priests and bishops for their deliverance. His words were measured and occasionally blunt but never course or undermining.

William's letter was sent to Aylesbury News, the same paper that had previously published the vicar's monologue. By now, the editor had taken a personal interest in the discourse and made the following comments, in the paper, about both men.

He called the vicar's letter derisive and said 'that by the use of language and slang phrases anyone would think that he had been educated at Billingsgate.' (A fish market in London). When in fact he was educated at Oxford.

The reverend replied in a sarcastic tone:

'I feel honoured by your notice of my pamphlet, and your little abuse of me: it is better than an advertisement which I never wished and never courted.'

Of William, the editor said,

'Although Mr Hopcraft has not had the advantage of a classical education, he displays a much better knowledge of the Scriptures, and the spirit which ought to be shown by a Christian minister, than his antagonist.'

William's true character was here for all to see. He stood up for the truth and did not allow himself to be bullied by someone who thought himself superior. He was an intelligent, God-fearing man who was diligent, fair and conscientious.

This was the oppression, challenge and obstacle with which William had to contend. The two men lived half a mile apart and came across each other's paths on a regular basis but Thomas never accepted William in his role as minister. It had been many years since it was legal to practice religion away from the state church but the prejudice remained.

William would not live to see it but time did not soften his antagonist and some thirty years later, he was still being hostile towards the Baptists in the name of religion. It was quite a shocking incident and worthy of note. It was 1855, and a new Baptist chapel in the centre of the village was being built. The vicar was more than unhappy with this turn of events and organised a protest. He gathered around him a group of supporters and set off in procession around the village and towards the building site. They pushed a cart around with them containing an effigy of a calf stuffed with straw, representing the Baptists, implying that they were serving a false God. The calf was placed on the ground where the church hall now stands and was dramatically set on fire with their leader ranting and prophesising that the new chapel would soon be used as a barn. (The building still stands today and is home to a wonderful, welcoming congregation of spirit-filled Christians).

Disease and death were constant companions as William ministered to the local people. The health of the village was supervised by the overseers of the poor but there was no local doctor or nurse and people often had to fend for themselves. In 1831, the worst of the cholera epidemics in England began. It reached Crendon by June 1832 causing many deaths. Whole families were wiped out and many parents who survived lost their children. At the beginning of the epidemic, a father brought his child, one of the first to die, to the grave on a truck. He was walking the path of grief alone without a single follower for support. Everyone was afraid for their lives and for the lives of their loved ones. By the next year, the disease had run its course but had left much heartache in its wake.

In 1836, Emma (my great great grandmother) was born to Mary and William's son Joseph and his wife Sarah. The young couple already had a busy life with a houseful of children but within months, Sarah found she was pregnant again. Joseph, much like his father before him, had to work hard to keep a roof above their heads and food on the table and this unexpected pregnancy added to his pressure.

He was desperately trying to keep his head above water when tragedy struck. Maybe, he was overworked or was in the wrong place at the wrong time, either way, he was an active man one day but laid low the next. Joseph had contracted typhus fever.

The privies (toilets) in the gardens of the cottages were a major source of the disease. They were communal with often only one provided, for a row of houses. They regularly overflowed, with their stagnating stench pervading the air. The sewerage emanated out, mixing with the rotting vegetable waste thrown from the back doors, creating a cesspit of invisible germs. It was another disease with the potency to devastate. One man in the village lost fourteen children and grandchildren within weeks.

Everyone hoped that Joseph was strong enough to be one of the ones to overcome but William had seen too many deaths from typhus and knew that the odds were stacked against his son surviving.

Everything that could be done was carried out but the sickness progressed over days. His symptoms became worse, until his body could take no more and he breathed his last breath. Joseph was thirty-seven. He left behind his pregnant wife and four children who had been relying on him to put food in their bellies and clothes on their backs. History was repeating itself.

Sarah was devastated. The man she loved had been stolen from her without notice. He had taken with him her emotional, financial and practical support and any dreams they had for a better future. She had been left to cope with 4 children, and another one on the way. Like many women in the community, she was a lace maker but that alone was not enough to sustain her family.

It was a bitter blow for William and Mary. Their eldest son had been taken. The child they had raised and loved; a young man who had everything to live for, gone in a blink of an eye. They missed him, and for William, the sad faces of his fatherless grandchildren were a stark reminder of his own childhood. However, Joseph had left part of himself behind, and the next year Sarah went into a long labour giving birth to not one but two girls, Sarah and Ann. There were now twins in the family.

The Finishing Line

William was getting older. His walk was not quite as brisk and his voice not so strong but he was resolute as he carried on with his ministerial duties. His usual sermons were interspersed with invites to participate in other church events. On the 16th May 1838, he was welcomed to a nearby village to preach to a crowded room of over one hundred people as they celebrated the arrival of a new vicar. After the service, they were all treated to an afternoon tea, costing them six pence each.

Long Crendon Baptist Chapel had for a long time, been part of the Buckinghamshire Association. It had formed in 1811, composed of several churches in the county. In this way, there was accountability, support, spiritual unity and shared vision. The church at Haddenham village, four miles away, was part of the association. Its minister, Mr Tyler, was a close friend of William and remained so for all of his life.

As a group, they campaigned together, drawing up petitions against several issues including slavery and child labour, particularly the problem of young chimney sweeps that often lost their lives in the course of their work. They were politically aware; focussed on changing England's socio-economic climate of the time.

The association met once a year and in 1841, William took his turn to host and chair the annual two-day event. The meeting started promptly at 1 pm on Tuesday the 11th May. The whole afternoon was spent in matters of church business including approving a circular letter that was ready to be printed and distributed to the Baptist community, entitled 'On caring for the souls of others'.

The sixteen-page letter began with the following statement.

'We believe it to be a fact, that every man is the possessor of a soul of infinite value; it being of an intelligent and immaterial nature, capable of knowing, loving and serving God…it is also believed by us, that the souls of men are in danger of being eternally lost…and this as the sad result of sin. "all have sinned and come short of the glory of God."'

It then went on to elaborate on this before giving the anecdote of salvation.

> For God so loved the world that He gave His one and only Son, that whoever believes in Him shall not perish but have eternal life. (John 3:16)

This was followed by an encouragement to care for others' souls. The heading titles included,

Human agency is instrumental in saving souls.
To care for the souls of others is peculiar to the Christian.
This duty is dictated by a spirit of benevolence.
For this purpose, talents are given to the Christian.
Let your pious care extend to the neighbourhood in which the providence of God has placed you.
You have also to care for the world at large.

All of which were expounded upon in detail.

A section on prayer and the importance of their social prayer meetings was included. It was not a popular meeting with many people 'having the opportunity but not the inclination to attend.' So a question was asked. If you care for the souls of others, then why are you not meeting with other Christians in order to pray for the salvation of the lost? It was quite a challenge, along with an instruction. Attend that you may pray.

As part of their conclusion they wrote,

'Finally, dear brethren, we would affectionately remind you, that whatever you resolve to do for the good of souls and the advancement of the Saviour's cause must be done promptly.'

There was a genuine, heartfelt compassion for lost souls and it was their desire to see as many saved as possible, aware that time was short.

When the meeting came to its conclusion, all the visiting ministers left to stay overnight at the Eight Bells inn (named after the number of bells at the parish church) located in the High Street, not far from William's house. The proprietor of the premises, George, was a familiar face to them as he welcomed them in for the night with a cheery smile and a cup of ale.

At seven o'clock the next morning, they met with William, at the church, for a time of prayer and praise, followed by a sermon on Romans 8:16:

> The Spirit Himself testifies with our spirit that we are God's children.

It was a beautiful verse to focus on. The Holy Spirit bears witness and confirms to everyone who is led by the Spirit that they are child of God; adopted into His royal family and joint heirs with Jesus. William had no doubts that he was a precious child of God.

After the sermon, they enjoyed lunch before commencing with a public meeting for the whole congregation and any visitors that wished to attend. Each represented church read out a letter to inform and interest the assembly. An extract from William's letter read:

'The additions to our church this year have been principally from the Sabbath School. The teachers have experienced a reviving influence, and are proceeding as persons sensible of their responsibility, and there is no doubt but their labours have been blessed.'

At the end of the day, the gathering came to a close. It was agreed that the meeting had been both solemn and interesting and that a delightfully harmonious spirit had prevailed.

The whole event had been a success and William could breathe a sigh of satisfaction and relief as he made his way back to Mary and the home they had shared since their wedding day. It was a lot less crowded these days as all but two of their children had moved out, settling in the village with growing families of their own. Some of them had kept tradition and followed in their father's footsteps becoming accomplished tailors and seamstresses. One of their sons set himself up as a baker, no doubt serving all the Nonconformists. William would never again be short of freshly baked bread.

William, now sixty-five, and Mary, sixty-seven, had lived selfless lives with very little time for themselves. Raising a family had been demanding and rewarding but the sudden loss of their son had deeply affected them. Mary's grief slowly gave way to an unending tiredness and by the next year, her mortal time had come to an end. She had lived a busy, purposeful life, dedicated to God's work but now it was time for her to rest.

William was distraught. She had been his constant companion and support for nearly 45 years and he missed her. He missed the sound of her voice and her beautiful smile. There was a big empty space where she had always been. The love of his life had gone and he would never be the same again.

Despite his grief, William was faithful. He put his heartache aside, only to be contemplated on in the stillness and silence of night. He continued on with God's work. He was still planting seeds in other places, sending twelve members of his congregation to form a church five miles away at Oakley, the place where they had initially set up a Sabbath School. The meetings were held in a little cottage with William travelling there by horse and cart every Sunday after his morning sermon. He would preach to the congregation in Oakly, before returning to conduct the service at Long Crendon in the evening.

His stamina was remarkable, but despite his will power and determination, the loss of Mary continued to distress him and his health began to fail. The joint in his knee began to swell, causing him issues and limiting his mobility. Soon after, his whole constitution began to be affected and his body started to deteriorate. Nevertheless, despite his weakness and frailty, he continued to preach three times every Sunday, missing only two services due to his condition.

Inevitably, the sad day came when he stood at his pulpit to preach his last ever sermon. The occasion was a sober one. As he spoke, his ashen face and trembling body left no one in any doubt that his death was near but he remained there with all the perseverance and strength that he had always shown. He wanted to give his flock one last message and he chose a very fitting verse for his last preach. Psalm 85:9:

> Surely His salvation is near those who fear Him, that His glory may dwell in our land.

The room was silent as they listened to their pastor's last words from the pulpit: a pulpit that he had guarded well. He was candid and talked about his death, saying:

'I wonder how I should feel when I come to be laid on a bed of affliction with my children and friends around me.'

The general agreement at the end of the service was that he spoke very impressively and affectionately.

He shut the church door for the last time, and went back to his house where he took to his bed for about 3 weeks. He began to rally slightly and there was even a prospect that he might recover but it was a vain hope. His suffering continued until his frame could take no more and on the morning of Thursday 8th May, his spirit departed his body. William Hopcraft had gone to his Father's house where there was a place waiting for him.

John 14:1-3:

> Do not let your hearts be troubled. You believe in God believe also in me. My Father's house has many rooms; if that were not so, would I have told you that I am going there to prepare a place for you? And if I go and prepare a place for you, I will come back and take you to be with me that you also may be where I am.

Six days later, his good friend and brother in Christ, Peter Tyler from Haddenham, conducted the funeral. The lonely wooden coffin, set in pride of place, brought sadness and sobriety to the heart of the chapel that had meant so much to William. It was a personal goodbye from Peter, as he addressed the congregation speaking affectionately about William's life and all he had achieved in the name of Jesus. His ministry had been prosperous and although it was a sorrowful day, there was also much to celebrate.

After the formalities, he was buried, not in the cemetery but respectfully beneath the pulpit where he had shared his final sermon. A marble tablet was erected to his memory.

> In memory of Mr William Hopcraft, who died May 8th 1845 aged 69 years. He was the faithful and highly esteemed pastor of this church for 23 years. "be thou faithful unto death and I will give thee a crown of life" Revelation 2:10.

William had touched many lives and his ministry had been fearless and fruitful. This was the end of William's life on Earth; no longer would his wise counsel and Godly wisdom be heard on the streets or in the church. No more would his smile brighten up someone's day. His children had lost a loving father and his grandchildren a benevolent and trusted Grandpa. His friends mourned their loss and his congregation missed him deeply.

It was a melancholy day for those left behind but for William it was a release from all the temporal things of the world, he had been liberated from all the trials that life had given him. For many years, he had been free in spirit but now he was free from the shackles of his human body. He had been consistently faithful in the face of hardship and persecution and now he had his promised reward...a crown of life.

Philippians 1:21-23:

> For to me, to live is Christ and to die is gain. If I am to go on living in the body, this will mean fruitful labour for me. Yet what shall I choose? I do not know! I am torn between the two: I desire to depart and be with Christ, which is better by far.

William had lived his life well and I like to think that he would be greeted in the next life by the words:

'Well done, my good and faithful servant.'

But this is not the end of the story. Death is never the end. William had lived out God's plan for him during his time on Earth. He had been obedient and conscientious and God had used him to be part of His plan to bring light into a dark place, a plan to draw people to the Kingdom. However, this was only part of God's design because He works on so many levels; some seen and others concealed. During William's lifetime, he had unwittingly been leaving a legacy for generations to come: a legacy that God led me to uncover at a time in my life when its significance would mean the most.

PART TWO
Catherine's Story

New Life

God knew me before I was born. All the days ordained for me were written in His book before I was even conceived. He has always had a plan for my life and part of that plan was to discover William's story in order to enrich my own.

My birth in 1961 was greeted with joy - a playmate for Richard, my two-year-old brother. Our family was now complete. The birth, compared to my mum's first labour was relatively easy but the pregnancy had been difficult. My father was a sergeant in the British military; billeted at an army base in Iserlohn, Germany. It had been quite an adventure for a young country girl to leave everything that was familiar, to follow her husband, on her first experience of going abroad.

The last twenty years of her life had been safe and sheltered but now my mum was in a strange country with a lively toddler, no family, few friends and limited knowledge of the local language.

When she became pregnant, she initially suffered from severe *morning* sickness that denied its name, continuing relentlessly throughout days and nights that blurred into each other. By the end of the first trimester it lifted and she felt well enough to travel back to England with Richard, to visit her mum and dad for a much-needed holiday.

Her parents were delighted to have her home; her dad had a soft spot for his little grandson, giving him lots of attention to make up for lost time. With eleven siblings in the locality, my mum did not have a minute to spare; lots of people to see and news to catch up on. She was enjoying being back until, one day, out of the blue, she began to feel ill. As the hours went on she started to feel progressively worse, until it was deemed necessary to send for the local doctor. It did not take him long to conclude that all was not well. He told her that for the sake of her health, she should not continue with the pregnancy. The news was distressing but it did not come as a complete shock as she knew the pregnancy was risky. My brother's birth had been very difficult, leaving her exhausted and ill and she had been told not to ever consider having any more children, as it was too dangerous for her.

My mum listened quietly to the doctor's advice, knowing she had to make a decision. The truth is my parents had taken the hospital's initial warning seriously and my conception had come as a surprise and a conflicting blessing. It was not an easy decision but she was married to a supportive man, and so she chose, against medical advice, to continue with the pregnancy.

She was ordered to rest, with her dad insisting she go to bed, while her parents looked after her and Richard. It was a while before she was able to travel but in due time she was fit enough to make the journey back to Germany, to await my arrival. She said her fond farewells not knowing it was to be the last time she would see her dad. Before she returned, he would suffer a fatal heart attack while taking one of his grandsons to the allotment at the back of his house.

The next few months were difficult; hours of apprehension, not knowing what the final outcome would be but also many moments of expectation, hoping for the best. Although the pregnancy was traumatic, the birth turned out to be less problematic. We both survived the ordeal and I entered the world in the early hours of a cold, snowy January, weighing five pounds and four ounces: a girl to complete the family.

As I grew up, one of my comedic relatives would often joke and call me Miss Stake. He was just being humorous because I was an unexpected child but I now know I was not a mistake. I was always meant to be. God created me in my mother's womb; He wove me together like a beautiful tapestry. He knew me when I was hidden in that secret place and He knows me now. My days are in His hands; they always have been.

Unlike William, I was born into a clean, safe environment, wrapped in soft, hand-knitted, with love, clothes and a cosy white heirloom shawl. Not for my pampered skin, the rough black wool blanket, straight off the spinning wheel, of the nineteenth century. We were given time to bond together as mother and daughter, during our customary ten-day stay in hospital, unlike William's mother Ann, who had meals to cook and work to do within hours of giving birth.

My parents at the time were anti-religion and chose to skip the expected traditional christening. God was not going to be allowed to have any part in my life! When I first learnt that they had deprived me of my *naming and blessing* ceremony, I was upset but the fact is they did not make promises that they were not prepared to keep. They did not bow to society just for a superficial day of show and celebration and for that, I am grateful. They loved and cherished me and that was more than enough.

William, on the other hand, had been christened in a cold austere church based on convention and ritual. Neither of us had a public party to welcome us into the world, no fancy frills or silver spoons and not a silk gown to be seen between us. God, however, had both of us in His sights from before we were born. Each of us destined for a different time and for diverse days but intrinsically linked by God's purpose for our lives.

When I was eighteen months old, my dad left the army to re-join *Civvy Street*. The whole family packed our respective bags and moved back to England to settle in Redditch, the hometown of both my parents: a town that I would live in for the next fifty-five years.

My dad was a hard worker and always provided but, for many years of my childhood, life was financially testing. Yet, in comparison to William's childhood, I was rich without measure. I cannot fully comprehend the poverty that William and his family went through.

My parents never had to make the decision whether to pay rent or put food on the table. I did not have to work to earn pennies by the time I was five. My occupation was playing with my dolls and a china tea set. I have never had that gnawing feeling in the pit of my stomach, not knowing when I was going to eat again. My mum was an amazing cook and, despite working full time in a factory, she would cook up a fabulous dinner from scratch every day. Her apple pies on a Sunday were the highlight of my week.

We had the money for basics but not for extras. At times, I had to miss out on much anticipated school day-trips because the funds were not there. Those around me seemed to have more than I did. I always wanted a pushbike but my parents could never afford one so I had use of my mum's old bike that was heavy and cumbersome and mortifyingly old fashioned. Sometimes we even had to use torn up newspapers for toilet roll, - that was an imprint I will not forget.

My parents both worked long hours; I was a latch key child, letting myself into an empty house after school and, at other times, visiting friends to share their after school treats. Most of my clothes were beautifully homemade apart from my seventies staple of cheesecloth and jeans. I never frequented a hairdresser and everything was used again or adapted to another purpose; my mum was a war child and she had learnt to be thrifty.

My parents grew their own vegetables and made their own wine from the dandelions that I was sent out to pick! Gifts were never extravagant but given with so much love. We walked - we walked a lot and once a year we had a camping holiday, near the mountains, creating precious memories, usually in the rain.

I knew what it was to be cold. We lived without much warmth for many years. On bitter winter mornings, I would marvel at Jack Frost's patterned antics and the icicles hanging on the inside of the window. My rough blankets were heavy and sometimes damp but I had a special one that my gran had brought me. It was pink with a satin edge. It was luxurious, to me, as I rubbed my chin against the soft material, feeling like a princess. Shivering I would run downstairs, despite my chilblains, to get dressed in front of the blazing open-fire; the only source of heat in the house. As a teenager, it was one of my jobs to light the fire when I came home from school. I never did fully master the complexities of the craft and was very relieved when gas central heating was installed.

I never had the privilege of going to Sunday School and God was never mentioned in our house. At school, we had to learn the Lord's Prayer off by heart and recite it, with our hands folded and eyes shut, at the end of the day before we left for home. I was good at reciting and would take pleasure in running through the words twice as fast to see if I could get through the prayer two times, before everyone else finished; taking great delight in making my friends laugh. Religion, faith, whatever you call it, meant nothing to me. God was just a fictional figure in my head with no relevance to my little life at all.

Spiritual Awakening

God was of no relevance, that is, until I was twelve and my wonderful grandmother became ill. She had fallen while collecting the washing off the line, and broken her hip. She never fully recovered and after leaving hospital, she was bed-bound, becoming more and more fragile until death made its presence known.

I loved my kind, generous, warm, loving gran so much, and when my mum rushed off in the hope of seeing her mother one last time, I felt my heart dissolving; my happiness bubble had burst. I walked down to the bottom of the garden and considered the God that I prayed to every school afternoon and decided I would ask Him for help. I somehow knew He was the only one that could mend the situation.

I uttered my first meaningful prayer and asked God to save her and not let her die. A few hours later, my mum came home and told me that my grandmother had passed away. The prayer had not worked but I do not think I had really believed it would. The truth is I now know that there is a season for everything under the sun and it was her time to go.

Later that night, I crawled into bed and lay on my back looking up into darkness as silent tears slid down the sides of my face. Apart from a stray cat that had died on me, I had no experience of death. It was not something that was ever talked about or that I had ever thought about until then. My precious grandmother was gone and now I had to face the reality that one day my parents would die and I would be on my own - it hit me hard. The tears continued.

The house was silent until I heard a voice call my name. *Cathy, everything is going to be alright.* I sat up and listened hard but no one was up, the rest of the family were in bed and all was quiet. It was a definite audible voice and I became convinced that somehow it was my grandmother speaking to me. Then an unfamiliar peace came over me; the peace invaded my body, deep down, somewhere unknown. I felt so comforted, like being hugged while wrapped up in a cosy blanket. I had a strong sensation of being loved. I felt secure and protected, floating in a new bubble, surrounded by warmth and safety.

I immediately came to terms with the situation and knew that everything would be alright. The tears stopped, leaving dry rivulets pasted to my cheeks; the only evidence left of my previous turmoil. I turned over and went to sleep.

When I woke in the morning, I still had that feeling of stillness and tranquillity, deep down inside of me. I had no idea then but I now know, without doubt, that my Heavenly Father was reaching down to comfort me. Just like William, when he turned to the wall and had an experience of God, after the death of his dad when he was twelve years old. That incredible, healing gift from God stayed with me for a few weeks until it gradually faded away, so quietly, that I did not even notice it going.

Life continued routinely; my time taken up with friends, school, reading and the menagerie of pets that I had accumulated. I was growing up, slowly leaving my childhood thoughts behind me as I looked to the future. It never occurred to me to pray to God again or even consider His existence. My life was okay. I was quite happy, thank you.

Surprisingly, my dad owned a family Bible that had been sitting on the shelf, collecting dust, for as long as I could remember. It was a big, heavy King James edition and I remember curiosity getting the better of me as I pulled it out one day. I laid it on the floor and sat down to look at it. There was a lot of writing but at the end of every section, there were beautiful old fashioned pictures. I spent time poring over the images, fascinated by them, trying to work out the stories behind each illustration. As I turned the pages, I came across some gruesome death scenes of Jesus on the cross with Mary cradling Him, as He lay dead in her arms. I had no concept of who Jesus was, nevertheless, it sparked something in me and I was drawn to gaze at those images again and again.

The one thing that did stay with me was an awareness of death; I had forgotten about the reassurance I had received when my grandmother had passed away and, possibly, the sight of Jesus bleeding and dying on the pages of the Bible, fed my fears. Night after night I would think about death and its consequences; the tears would soak my pillow and I felt scared. I was fearful of my own mortality and that of my family but by the morning, my anxieties would ebb away just as the moon gives way to the light of the sun as the darkness dispels.

The seasons came and went and I changed from a child to a young woman. I always had a sense that there was something more; a piece of the puzzle was missing for me but I did not know what it looked like, until I had my second encounter with God. When I was thirteen our cousin invited my brother along to a Bible class for teenagers. The venue was an old Brethren Gospel Hall. I noticed his absence on a Sunday morning but did not really think much about it until one afternoon when he walked into our lounge with a couple who were about the same age as my parents.

I carried on with my ironing until they explained they had come to see me. They wanted to know if I wanted to join them on a Sunday. I felt flattered so I put the iron down and thought about it. Why not? It was something to do. I had to get my parents' permission - they were a little reticent at first but they ultimately said yes. A few weeks later, I was in a room with a motley, spotty looking crew, listening about things in the Bible that I had never heard of before.

I loved the stories! I found it all a bit complicated, but it was a revelation to me that God had written His own book to guide us morally. I was very much like young William at this point. I was enthusiastic about this new way of looking at things – I wanted to obey the rules but it was difficult to understand. I enjoyed going and made a few superficial friendships but it was hard to fit in. Most of the children there were from Christian families and I was an outsider. Despite this, I was drawn to finding out more, and continued with my Sunday morning dip into the Word of God.

I eventually found my place in the group and started to have fun. We had lots of social evenings and parties at our leaders' home. I have cherished memories of those times. Gordon and Audrey Moores are wonderful people and I thank God for the blessing they have been in my life. They cared deeply for the youth in the church, giving up their time and energies so freely for us but, most importantly, they shared the Gospel. We would laugh, eat, play games and talk about this man Jesus who had died for us, for me. The flame had been lit and a light began to glimmer.

The banner at the front of the Gospel Hall read

> For God so loved the World that He gave His only begotten Son, that whosoever believes in Him should not perish but have everlasting life.

I had no idea what *begotten* was but the everlasting life bit really appealed to me. This could be a solution to my night-time fears. The words became stamped on my mind but, for a while, that is where they stayed.

In the summer of that same year, a barbeque was organised for the youth of the area. A Christian singer armed with guitar and long hair played to a captivated audience. At the end of the evening, he put down his instrument and made a simple appeal. He asked us to pray a prayer, and raise our hand, if we wanted to ask forgiveness for our sins and to commit our life to Jesus. I raised my hand. At this point, I think I expected something to happen but there were no thunderbolts, in fact there was nothing. I did not feel any different. I went home and kept quiet about the decision I had made that night.

I continued going to church, sometimes even twice on a Sunday but like William, I too had opposition and alienation from various quarters. One of my school friends saw me walking up the hill carrying my Bible and taunted me with the words *Bible basher*. In response, I became embarrassed and hid my Bible under my coat. I was hardly a defender of my faith! Someone in my family who had Bible knowledge but no knowledge of Jesus delighted in arguing with me about the 'inconsistencies' in The Word and I would get myself tied up in knots trying to give an explanation but failing abysmally.

Despite these setbacks, my newfound faith manifested a desire in me to do something practical to show I was different. I joined the school's Christian club (for about a month) and proudly wore a yellow badge with the words 'Smile, Jesus Loves You.' In 1974, when the film The Exorcist came to our local cinema I marched up there, with an agenda to *enlighten* anyone who would listen. I walked up and down the waiting queue, handing out leaflets in an attempt to dissuade people from opening themselves up to evil. Looking back, I had also caught William's early *pious bug*.

Today, I would still strongly encourage others not to open themselves up to any form of dark, satanic influence. The difference now is that I do not have my teenage self-righteous attitude. Back then, I thought I had all the answers, when in reality my knowledge and understanding was a thin veneer of second-hand information.

About a year later, a friend came into my life who attended a church of a different religion. She invited me to come along, and in my gullibility, I joined her. They had completely different beliefs to me and I began to listen to counter arguments against the deity of Christ, against the Trinity, against the existence of the Devil and against the power of the Holy Spirit. I tried to argue back in a way that Paul would not have approved of and guess what happened; I began to be drawn in. My faith began to waver and I jumped ship.

They were kind to me and I made new friends. I started to believe the lies. I had found a new spiritual home. If only I had read the Bible more and understood about false doctrines, I could have saved myself a lot of heartache.

I joined their youth group, enjoying the free food and activities they put on for us. One night they split us up into two equal groups. One side was the *For* group, and the other the *Against* group. Each week we were given a topic to discuss and we had to present our arguments to the leaders. We then had to vote on which group was right, I now realise it was all set up so that we would come out with the outcome that coincided with the belief of the church.

One week, I was in the *We don't believe in the Devil* group and I had to present arguments against his existence. I did it but I was so confused with the result. Apparently, the Devil had no place in the world; the source of anything and everything bad came from us. Of course, my group was considered correct but I was so perplexed. I went home and pored over my Bible, well into the night. I had a Bible that linked verses and I went from one to the other, with an ever-increasing belief that the Devil had to exist – in my mind there was no other explanation.

Knowing that they had misled me with one thing made me think that maybe they were wrong about everything else. I looked up the Trinity: God in three persons. It was a difficult concept to understand and I don't remember how or where I came up with the idea but I likened it to a glass of water – when it was frozen it was God, when it was fluid it was Jesus and when it was steam it was the Holy Spirit. Bingo! It all made sense and it suddenly hit me that this too was true.

I left their church and rushed back to the safety of the Gospel Hall. I had strayed but now I was back. Unfortunately, some damage had been done and I had a lot of *undoing* to go through. Like William, I had taken on board false beliefs about Jesus and God, and all it had done was to make me depressed and mixed-up.

New Beginnings with One Foot in the World

Over the next five years, I continued learning about God and His ways. I grew into a young adult, living two separate lives. I now know it was my flesh fighting against my spirit but at the time, it was bewildering. It was hard to stay on the straight and narrow path when the world offered me so much. There were things to be enjoyed, new experiences to be had. Jesus was absolutely not the centre of my life – I was. I still believed in Him and was very grateful that I had been given everlasting life but it was a baby belief. I was still living on milk and not on solid food.

Slowly but surely I began to understand more about living the Christian life. It was still only part of me but I knew I could never turn my back on Jesus. I left school at 18 and was about to embark on the adventure of university so before I left, I chose to get baptised, encouraged by the words of Mark 16:16:

> Whoever believes and is baptized will be saved, but whoever does not believe will be condemned.

I thought I needed to believe *and* be baptised to safeguard my gift of eternal life and so I took the plunge. In the same way as William, I was baptised in the name of the Father, the Son and the Holy Spirit. I was lacking in confidence and so this public declaration was quite an ordeal. There was no fanfare of angels (that I could see!) It was significant but in a quiet, deep down way, stirring my heart but not shaking it. I did it as a step of obedience and as a witness to my faith but I felt very little difference in my daily life. The sad truth is I still had one foot in Heaven and the other foot solidly on the Earth. I was given a verse on my baptism day from Romans 8:28:

> And we know that in all things God works for the good of those who love Him, who have been called according to His purpose.

It was a verse that, at the time, had little significance but one that would come to be very precious to me in years to come.

I did not enjoy my university years. After the first term, having missed six weeks, because of contracting glandular fever, I wanted to leave. My decision to drop out did not go down well with anyone and I was persuaded to go back and make a go of it. It was difficult. My self-confidence was at low ebb and I was an introvert in an environment that did not have room for me.

I still had a desire to prove my worth as a Christian and in order to facilitate my need I joined Amnesty International. Jesus was all about human rights. He always stood up for the underdog. One of the ways I could help was to write letters to those in authority, to try to make a difference. I enjoyed the challenge to help people in dire need and imagined the positive responses to my pleas and demands. It opened my eyes up to the injustice in the world and the plight of so many people. I was very naïve in my initial efforts to change the trajectory of inequality and discrimination.

I was expecting overnight success and quickly had to alter my expectations. The realisation of the brokenness on the planet I called home and man's inhumanity to man impacted my soul and created a deep compassion within me. As a person, I grew a lot during my time as a member of Amnesty International, but in terms of deep spiritual growth, it was a distraction, albeit, a very worthwhile one.

As a result of my awakening to the chaos in the world, I became quite introspective and sad. I began writing poetry in an attempt to express myself. I soon discovered that it was not my gifting. Nevertheless, the words exposed my state of mind. I knew that without God, we were all lost. I wrote a poem reflecting these thoughts.

Life Without God

An Earth remoulded, sorry state
Upon that distant sky
The dark and dismal air of pain
Within each frightened eye

The world, so sure in distant past
Is but a blessed dream
And echoes of a child's laugh
Rise cruelly to be seen

So on an ancient face of love
The maggots tear at flesh
And wings that soared the peaceful dove
Now strain to break life's mesh

Sad winds that once refreshed her ground
Lay dormant, without calm
And footsteps, once with joyous sound
Drag slowly, yet with harm

For with each step her people take
Another notch is scored
Another race, its history lost
Another boat is moored

And on that distant skyline
We all prepare to flee
We all receive a second look
But our future's never free

I ran out of inspiration after penning about a dozen equally depressing poems and gratefully closed the chapter on a particularly melancholy stage of my life.

On the 29th July 1981, instead of joining in the celebrations of the wedding of Charles and Diana, I was invited to a Campaign for Nuclear Disarmament (CND) meeting It was a beautiful day and after the speeches were over we enjoyed a very civilised garden party. Again, I felt I was doing something to make a change for the better. I had grown up with the dread of a nuclear war, always there in the background. Nuclear mushroom pictures were imprinted on my mind and I was fearful for the future.

I became involved in campaigns for several good causes, spending my time getting petitions signed and doing my best to *educate* people. I realise now, I was desperately trying to be a *good* person. I believed that I was pleasing God by all my practical efforts, when in truth I should have been kneeling at His feet.

Then came the *wilderness* years: not in the sense of sex, drugs and rock & roll, but a spiritual wilderness. I was walking around the desert in circles looking for a way home. They were the longest years in terms of time but the least significant in terms of growth, although I wouldn't be where I am today without them.

I completed my degree, got married, had two beautiful children, got divorced and married again. I then suffered a traumatic miscarriage that resulted in another *God moment*.

It was spring 1994. I was pregnant and felt on top of the world. I had only been married for five months and the pregnancy was a bit of a surprise but I was thrilled with the idea. I felt really well and had so much energy. I had even started making preparations for *housing* our new arrival. Then on a Saturday night, I began to feel unwell. We called the doctor and he confirmed our worst fears – it looked as if I was about to miscarry. I was ordered to stay in bed but the situation grew progressively worse. The next day, ironically, it was Mothers' Day, I was taken into hospital. A scan revealed that the baby had died and it was decided that I needed to go down to theatre.

I had kept myself together up to this point but hearing a doctor spell it out in black and white was just too much to cope with. The minute the doctor had gone I broke down, sobbing and talking incoherently. Why had my body let me down? Why was I unable to sustain this tiny life? Had I done something wrong? What would happen to the soul of my baby? My emotions were racing and the noise and the smells of the hospital were strange and frightening. My head began to rage with pain and I started to be violently sick.

The nurses tried to steady me, telling me that theatre would have to be delayed if I did not calm down. As most of us do in an hour of need, I called on God. I asked my husband to pray for me. He held my hand and quietly prayed for God to be with me and for the reality of God to touch my life.

It was at this point that I felt a warm glow begin to creep into my body. It started like gentle spring sun washing over me before becoming a powerful surging force of hot energy. I felt strong arms wrapped around me, and a quiet voice telling me that everything was going to be all right. I knew, without any doubt, that someone was there with me. My eyes were closed, with my husband still holding my hand, sitting beside me oblivious to my experience. Then slowly the presence moved away leaving me feeling complete; knowing that as the voice had said *everything was going to be all right.*

I turned and smiled at my husband, 'You can go now,' I said, 'I'll be fine.' It took a while to convince him that I would really be okay on my own but as it was now the early hours of the morning he reluctantly left me. About an hour later, the anaesthetist came to check me out and commented on how calm I was. 'No need for a pre-med,' he joked.

Within two years of this loss, by God's grace, I gave birth to another beautiful child. I now had a son and two daughters and my quiver was full. Life was busy. I was working, running a home, acting as taxi driver and doing all the things that society leads us to believe are beneficial to get on in this world. During which time, along with my husband, I attended several churches, taught in Sunday School and lived the best life I could.

My spiritual life on the other hand was, in many ways, only skin deep. I think I was literally just inside the outer edge of the Kingdom! I hardly ever prayed, rarely read the Bible and did not understand the deeper concept of what Christ had done for me: His sacrifice and His love.

Living in this cloud of spiritual mediocrity went on for many years. Up to this point my life journey had been complicated; I had been through a lot of negative experiences and I felt depressed and deeply sad; a Christian with a far from ideal existence but God wanted more for me. He began to gently prompt me until I came to the realisation that my relationship with Him had floundered and was on the rocks. I knew my life was spiralling out of control and there was only one person who could help – Jesus.

At the height of my depression, I spent the night pacing the kitchen floor repeating the beginning part of the verse I had been given at my baptism.

> Everything works together for good for those who love Christ Jesus.
>
> Everything works together for good for those who love Christ Jesus.
>
> Everything works together for good for those who love Christ Jesus.

I was a bit manic at the time but as I repeated the words over and over again, a calm came over me. Above all things, Jesus was calling me to love Him again, to love Him in a way I had never loved Him before. The only way my life could ever become a full life was to love Jesus with all my heart. I also realised that the verse I had been repeating had a second half. 'And we know that in all things God works for the good of those who love Him, who have been called according to His purpose.'

Was I called according to His purpose? Was I part of His plan? I came to the conclusion that I must be but it wasn't something that I had ever considered before. God was calling me to a deeper relationship with Him and I was starting to listen but He still had a few home truths to tell me.

The problem with superficiality is that it is what you see on the surface, not what is actually going on behind the scenes and, for most of us most of the time, we can get away with it. Particularly as Christians, we can say and do the right things but deep down where it counts, we can lack any real depth. God was about to show me where I was lacking and it was not going to be an easy lesson to take.

As I sat in a church, on a Sunday morning, doing my best to concentrate on the sermon, my mind suddenly became focused on something God was trying to tell me. Throughout my Christian journey, I had rarely received visions or pictures but this was the day that God chose to reach out in a visual way. In my mind, I saw a solid, red, old-fashioned thermos flask. God removed the lid. I walked over to the flask and peered inside to see what delicious drink was in store for me but the inner glass lining was broken, not just cracked but smashed into lots of tiny fragments. I tipped the flask over and out fell hundreds of tiny shards of glass. Then I heard the words, *you're a broken vacuum flask.*

I recognised where the words were coming from and knew God was speaking to me but that was it. There was no explanation and, for me, at that time, no real significance but the words stayed in my mind and kept coming back to me.

You're a broken vacuum flask. I kept praying and continued searching. Slowly, the meaning was revealed to me, step by step, until I understood what God was saying. A flask is a vessel with a specific job to do, just as I was a vessel with a task to accomplish.

On the outside, the flask looked perfectly good and in working order. In the same way, I looked okay on the outside. I appeared to be functioning and doing all the right things but inside I was not fit for purpose. I was broken. This was the essence of me – I was lying broken and damaged inside a phony, plastic image. The flask had one of two jobs. It was designed to keep liquid either hot or cold but now it could do neither. This was me. I was a sham. I was not hot. I was not cold. Spiritually I was lukewarm. The flask was red, the colour of blood and yes, I was covered by the blood of Christ but because

I had not allowed Him fully into my life to heal and restore, God could not use me for the purpose He had in mind.

It came as a shock when I realised that God was telling me that I was lukewarm. I knew the Bible had something to say about this. I went in search of His word and found Revelation 3:15-16:

> I know your deeds, that you are neither cold nor hot. I wish you were either one or the other! So, because you are lukewarm-neither hot nor cold - I am about to spit you out of my mouth.

This made me sit up and listen.

I still did not fully grasp the truth. I spent weeks trying to seek out wise guidance from other Christians. I bought self-help books and read them from cover to cover. I spent time in numerous counselling sessions. I tried in vain to mend my fractured mind - to become *whole* again but...I failed.

I prayed and God spoke to me again. The inside of the flask had broken into hundreds of tiny pieces, making it impossible for anyone to glue it back together again. It could never be restored to its former glory by human hands. Only God's hands could mend it, make it new again and fit for purpose.

I had a desire to *be fit for purpose*. I knew I had been sitting on the fence in many ways and I felt I was being given a choice. Hot or cold? Never lukewarm again. Later on, in the same chapter of Revelation God says:

> I correct and discipline everyone I love. So be diligent and turn from your indifference.

I was being admonished and called to obedience. I knew God loved me and I knew He had a design for my life. This was *make or break* time.

Growing

I was still a spiritual baby. I cried when I was hungry and screamed when I was thirsty; expecting somebody else to get the food and drink for me. I was undernourished to the point of malnutrition and I had done it to myself. I had been brought to my knees and I could wither up and die or I could start to drink, really drink, from the water He offered me. I could begin to eat solid food and start to grow up. My life had been given to Christ years ago but now I had a real desire to become mature in Him.

I wish I could report, at this point, that I prayed and I was transformed in a miraculous way. I believe God could have done that in a blink of an eye but chose not to. Had my spiritual and mental healing been that easy it would have meant little to me and would have had an insignificant affect on the rest of my life. God wanted me to be tested and tried so that my restoration would be complete. There was, and is, a spiritual battle being fought in Heaven and the journey was not going to be an easy one.

I needed to be unravelled, like a piece of knitting, to undo those missed stitches, to smooth out the knots in the wool so that I could be made complete again. Being unravelled is painful but being knit back up again is a joy.

The process began and one of the issues I identified was that I felt isolated. There had been times when I felt very alone as a Christian. It was my issue. I felt alienated and different, never unloved, but a sense that I did not really belong. I have an amazingly loving family who were, and are, the most important and precious earthly relationships in my life. It was not a physical loneliness. It was something intangible. I realised I felt spiritually alone. I wanted somebody in my family to think like me, to believe what I believed. I wanted to be able to have someone that understood how I felt; someone that recognised how important my faith was to me – how important God was to me. I wanted to feel I fitted in and for me that was in a spiritual sense. I also felt the burden of being the only one. I was mistaken in my understanding, but at the time, I felt solely responsible for the spiritual awakening of my children, my parents and therefore for the generations to come.

This sense of insecurity, of not belonging, was always with me and maybe, subconsciously, this was why I began dabbling in genealogy in my early twenties. It fascinated me to look back in history to see who my ancestors were and how they lived. I have spent hundreds of hours searching, discovering, collating and writing up the lives of those who went before me. I have jumped from branch to branch looking for that hidden something; putting all the pieces together like a jigsaw. I always had the feeling there was something I had not found yet, but I did not know who or what it was. I now know that I was looking for a spiritual connection, a spiritual tradition in my family, a sense of spiritual oneness.

I wanted to belong, but was looking in the wrong place and during my process of unravelling, God began to reveal to me that I already had a spiritual family. When I had accepted Jesus into my life, all those years ago, an adoption had taken place. I had been adopted into His household; I was a child of His and I was a joint heir with Jesus. It had been there all along but I had never acknowledged it. I had never understood the gift I had been given. God is my father and protector; Jesus is my brother and the Holy Spirit is my friend. They work together, as a family, to love, support and guide me but I had to want to be an active part of it.

Armed with this knowledge and experience, I no longer felt the need to rely on a family member for my heritage. My heritage was, and always had been, in God. If I was the only member of my biological family to follow Him, then so be it. I would stand up straight, hold my head high and remember whose daughter I was.

Then God stepped it up and spoke to me one Sunday morning. The minister was illustrating how our communication with God is sometimes blocked by all the rubbish that is in our lives. At times we do not hear clearly, because God is being filtered through all our junk. I don't remember anything else that the minister spoke about because at that point God gave me a vision – a picture – a daydream – call it what you want but it was from God. I cannot remember if my eyes were open or closed at the time but it took over my thoughts for the rest of the service.

I was looking on, as if watching a film. I could see myself distinctly. I was sat inside a cage; a prison cell measuring about ten feet by five. There were bars all around me and I could see clearly out into a bright, light world. The ground outside my prison cell was covered in golden, yellow sand; I was in the middle of a desert with nothing but sand dunes surrounding me. I was sat hunched up on a little stool and surrounding me were many bags of dirty, overflowing, smelly garbage. I could see steam rising from them, filling the air with a terrible stench. It was the odour of hurt, unforgiveness, unjustness and contrition. It was the aroma of sin: my sin and the sin of those people I had not been able to forgive.

The strange thing was, I seemed to be quite content for a while sitting amongst all the trash. I was used to it, it was comfortable and in a peculiar way had become my security blanket. I felt safe in my cell. The scary bit was outside in the big wide world. Then I looked up, and as I looked, Jesus appeared on the outside of my prison bars. I quickly realised that although I was comfortable here, it was not where Jesus was.

Jesus stood there outside my prison door, just looking at me as He pulled back the big heavy bolt that was keeping me locked in. There was no key just a bolt that I could have easily drawn back myself but I had chosen not to. He then stood back and waited. I remained seated thinking He will come and get me in a moment. He will come and take me away from all this rubbish. He will rescue me. However, Jesus just stood there looking at me and waiting. He never said a word.

Then it began to dawn on me that Jesus had already rescued me. He had died on the cross and given everything so that I could be free. Yet I was still trapped inside this prison because I had not fully grasped that freedom was there for the taking. He had offered me a fantastic gift. I had accepted it.

However, I had not unwrapped it. It was now up to me to remove myself from the despair I was in. I needed to be pro-active in accepting my freedom.

I stood up and taking one last look around, I walked up to the door and pushed. It opened easily. I walked outside towards Jesus. Then we both looked in through the bars of my cell in the desert, full of old dirty rubbish; rubbish I was now turning my back on. I turned and walked away with Jesus walking at my side. We walked up a steep sand dune with the grains sinking beneath my feet threatening to make me slip and slide back down. But, with Jesus next to me, I stayed upright and strong and continued walking forward.

As I looked ahead to the horizon, the light began to change. The only way I can describe it is the same type of experience you have when driving to the seaside. As you get nearer to the coast the light on the horizon changes and you know the sea is just over the next rise. It was that same type of light and I was filled with expectancy, not knowing what was on the other side of the hill but knowing that I was walking that way with Jesus and that it was going to be wonderful and beautiful. The promise was there. After a while, we stopped, turned around and looked back down the hill together. My prison cell could still be seen in the distance.

It had not disappeared but because I had walked so far with Jesus, my cell and all its contents had become insignificant in the landscape. Jesus was not going to make me forget. My memories were not going to be erased. It was up to me to walk away from my past. It is not how we fall that God is concerned with, it is how we get up that matters to Him. I am a new person my past is forgiven and everything is new.

It is a continuous walk. On occasions something happens, maybe a trigger to some past event that undermines my confidence and I find myself momentarily sat back in that desert cage, but I do not stay there. I walk through the door to join Jesus on the freedom side of my prison.

I began to heal. I felt truly secure for the first time in my life and all the behaviour and thoughts of the insecure person I had been, began to melt away. They were replaced by a need to be obedient and faithful at all costs.

My life became more disciplined. I began to be transformed. Romans 12:2 started to become a reality in my life.

> Do not conform to the pattern of this world, but be transformed by the renewing of your mind. Then you will be able to test and approve what God's will is - His good, pleasing and perfect will.

My mind was being repaired, restored, refreshed and renewed. It was a long process and a hard road to walk. I slipped. I stumbled. I fell, but Jesus was always there to pick me up, brush me down and set me in the right direction again.

Christ had died for me. By not accepting and living out the amazing offer of freedom that He had given me, I was throwing it back into His face. It was as if I had accepted the gift from Him, unwrapped it, used it for a bit and then wrapped it back up: never to be used and enjoyed again. God's plan was so much more than that for my life and so I unwrapped His gift completely and threw the paper away.

I had been a Christian for years but I still had much to learn. It is a bit like driving. When you first pass your driving test, you do all the right things for the first few weeks. You mirror and signal, before each manoeuvre. You know the theory and put it into practice. You stick to the rules totally focused on your surroundings but then, as you get more confident, you fall into bad, sloppy habits.

As a Christian, I had fallen into numerous slapdash habits because I was safe in the fact that I was saved. My prayer life was minimal and came from selfish desires. Reading the Bible had become a duty rather than a delight. I had been unaware of the bountiful blessings available to me, because I had not searched and gone deeper with God.

This was a time of digging down, unearthing treasures and drinking of His life-giving water. It was a time of recognising how little I knew and allowing God to mend the broken pieces of my life.

It was during this process of healing and growth that my life turned upside down. My beautiful mum who was my best friend and constant source of love and encouragement began to feel unwell. She was dizzy all the time and was diagnosed with labyrinthitis, an inner ear infection. She was told it was not serious but within three weeks, she was in hospital, with terminal cancer and a prognosis of two-three weeks to live. It was a complete shock for all the family but particularly my vibrant mum, who had so much energy and love for life.

There was no treatment available and so she came home and went down the holistic route, which gave her an extra six months. Throughout it all, she was strong and brave. She spent her time thinking of others, making sure that we would be okay when she was no longer with us. It was a bittersweet time. I gave up my job to help care for her and to spend as much time as I could, helping her to put things in order. There were days that I treasured and days that were a living nightmare but with God's strength, I was able to be with her to the end.

I had prayed impassioned prayers for my mum. I wanted her back to full health so that we could continue living life together. However, it wasn't to be. It was her time to go. When she died, I was full of grief and knew that my life and our family would never be the same again. It was hard to continue, in the way she would have wanted me to, with a smile on my face and a purpose in my walk. My children, despite their own heartaches, were incredible and bit by bit, we created a new way of living.

Jesus walked with me throughout the whole ordeal. He wrapped His arms around me and held me in the safety of His embrace. My faith never wavered. I recognised that God had it all in hand. My mum had accepted Jesus into her heart about ten years after I had first become a Christian. She knew and I knew where she was going and I have no doubt that one day we will be living another life together in eternity.

As a distraction to my sorrow, I began to continue with my family's genealogy. I picked up from where I had started a few years before and almost immediately, a remarkable thing happened. I came across my great, great, grandmother, Emma on my father's side. As a single mother who ran her own business, she fascinated me and I began to delve into her life. It was during this process that I encountered her grandfather, and my great great great great grandfather, William, who was a pastor and a Christian…and the rest is history.

We all have sixty-four great, great, great, great, grandparents and I do not believe it was a coincidence that I came across his path. I believe that God delayed revealing William to me until I felt secure and confident in God's family. Nevertheless, it was a wonderful revelation to find out that someone had gone before who would have understood me and my experiences.

As I began to learn about William's life, I found myself in personal condemnation - comparing myself against his quick growth into maturity. My previous joy began to dissipate and a dark cloud hung over me until God intervened and I realised two things. Firstly, our relationship with Jesus is personal. Each one of us has the opportunity for a unique experience and connection with Christ. We should never negatively compare our story with others. Secondly, I realised that William, who I had great respect for, was just as human as me.

I am proud of my biological heritage. I am proud of the man William was and I am honoured to be his great, great, great, great granddaughter but I am so much more honoured to be God's daughter. I am a daughter of the King.

Finding out about William came at a point in my life when I was safe in the knowledge that I was God's precious child. However, I believe God revealed my biological bloodline to me because He had much to teach me through the legacy that William left behind.

I was born one hundred and eighty-five years after William's birth and although in material ways, our lives could not have been more different, spiritually there are many similarities. The way he lived his life and the messages he gave have all had an impact on me. God has allowed a connection, through a biological bloodline, but so much more importantly, through the precious blood of Jesus Christ. William may be a grandfather figure to me but he is also my brother in Christ.

I can relate to William in a way I would not have thought possible. I never met him, I have no idea what he looked like; whether his eyes were blue or brown, if he was tall or short, if he smiled or frowned a lot. However, because of the writings left behind, I know, in part, how he thought and what was important to him. It is plainly clear that God was the central part of his world. He dedicated his life to teaching others about the saving grace of Jesus Christ.

PART THREE
God's Legacy Lessons

When I first began to read about William's life, I was fascinated with the differences between his world and my world. If I could step back in time to the first half of the nineteenth century, I would find it old fashioned, dull and restrictive and if he could see how we live now, I think he would believe he was in Sodom and Gomorrah.

There is a vast contrast in our attitudes, wealth, lifestyle and expectations. I thought our lives could not be further apart but as I began to look deeper, I discovered the similarities between us. He had experienced so many things that I could relate to. William had discovered a way of living a life that was honourable to God, despite his circumstances, and through his experiences and resolve, I could learn a lot.

I believe this was a continuation of the healing, growing, maturing process in me. There were new lessons to be taught and for those things that God had already revealed to me, William's teachings acted to give clarity and confirmation. This created in me, through the power of Christ, an anchor of steadfastness and discipleship.

His *classroom* was based in the early 1800s, while mine spanned twenty-two decades, with my lessons written on the slates of time. God's guidance reached me through William's words and actions, echoing my spiritual journey and mirroring my life. Two centuries of generations lay between us but God had gone before and prepared the way for a time when and I was ready to hear.

So God's legacy lessons began. William's writing's met with me personally and directly; they brought a sense of continuity and comfort. As I read his words, I believed they had been specifically written with me in mind. When I discovered the strength of his faith and his unwavering commitment to the cause, I thought it had been revealed to me for my personal edification and encouragement. It is indeed a special God-given gift, but William's memoirs, letters and spiritual story did not make their way into my hands just for my benefit. They needed to be revealed and communicated to others by putting pen to paper.

Throughout history, God has used the written word to share His plans and His thoughts.

Jeremiah 30:1:

> This is the word that came to Jeremiah from the Lord. This is what the Lord God of Israel says: Write in a book all the words I have spoken to you.

Habakkuk 2:2:

> Write down the revelation and make it plain on tablets so that a herald may run with it.

Romans 15:4:

> For everything that was written in the past was written to teach us, so that through the endurance taught in the Scriptures and the encouragement they provide, we might have hope.

I do not put myself in the same category of people like Jeremiah, but I know that the desire to write this book was laid on my heart by God and I have tried to be obedient to His call. There are lessons here that others, at some point, need to hear. It is in that belief, that I have undertaken and completed this book as one of God's blueprints for my life. I have no expectations for this book but trust that in my Father's timing, it lands in the laps and the hearts of the right people. I may never see this come to fruition and I do not need to. So many of our plans are time-bound but God is outside of time and I leave the exciting journey of these words in His capable hands.

His word is everlasting; it is the same today as it was yesterday and the same as it will be tomorrow.

Malachi 3:6:

> I the Lord do not change.

God is the one constant in our ever-evolving societies. He is dependable. He is truth and the words that applied to William all those years ago still apply to us now and in the future. Even though everything relentlessly moves on around us at such a pace, we can always rely on Scripture and God's eternal and immovable grace and love.

Legacy Lesson One
Relationship not Religion

Religion is the cause of so much chaos and confusion. I detest religion; to clarify, I loathe religion that is deceptive, particularly when it wears a mask of respectability in order to disguise the truth to the uninformed or unaware.

The Cambridge dictionary gives the following definition of religion:

'The belief in and worship of a god or gods, or any such system of belief and worship.'

This is the face that false religion has assumed. It wants the world to see it as following and venerating a higher being, for the good of humanity but its reality can be far from the truth.

William got caught up in religion as a young man. His search for truth was a direct consequence of his father's death. It is a common theme when we lose someone we love. It can spur us on to think about what happens to our loved ones when they die. This in turn, leads to fears about our own mortality and inquiries about life after death.

After searching for answers, William came to believe that what God required was for people to be pious. All that was needed in order to be acceptable in God's sight was for a person to be moral, dutiful and saintly and to do good deeds. It was all about the law, with a long list of do's and don'ts. It was a popular teaching, designed, no doubt, to keep people in 'their place.' This type of instruction often had the knock on effect of either producing sanctimonious, moralising bigots or creating such a heightened sense of sin in a person's life that it became an almost unbearable burden to carry.

William experienced both these reactions in his search for religion; each one causing him equal amounts of distress.

Colossians 2:8:

> See to it that no one takes you captive through hollow and deceptive philosophy, which depends on human tradition and the elemental spiritual forces.

William in his innocence and eagerness to discover the Gospel truth had been deceived. He had set out to find a resolve to his big questions but instead had been handed platitudes and bad attitudes and was at the mercy of man-made beliefs and practices.

William had walked unknowingly into a trap that many people have fallen into both before and after him. None of us can afford to be complacent. No one is safe from cultivating a 'religious' attitude. We need to actively protect our hearts and minds from such mind-sets and behaviours.

James 1: 26-27:

> Those who consider themselves religious and yet do not keep a tight rein on their tongues deceive themselves and their religion is worthless. Religion that God our Father accepts as pure and faultless is this; to look after orphans and widows in their distress and to keep oneself from being polluted by the world.

How many of us can truly say that we always keep a tight rein on our tongues? If we gossip, if our words are harsh, if we swear or shout, then our religion has become without value. True religion is to look after the most vulnerable in our society and to be in the world but not part of it. How often do we allow ourselves to be polluted by the world? How often do we put our needs second to help those less fortunate than us?

Jesus also had a few things to say about religion. In Mathew 23 He was talking to His disciples, along with a crowd of people. He advised them to follow the law of the Scriptures but not to imitate the actions of the Pharisees because they didn't practice what they preached.

In Matthew 23:4 Jesus said,

> They tie up heavy, cumbersome loads and put them on other people's shoulders, but they themselves are not willing to lift a finger to move them.

(Probably referring to the extra laws that had been fabricated to suit the leaders' needs and not part of God's word).

Jesus continued to be blunt on His opinion of the Pharisees. He spoke at length concerning seven woes regarding them. These included, 'Woe to you, teachers of the law and Pharisees, you hypocrites! You shut the door of the Kingdom of Heaven in people's faces. You yourselves do not enter, nor will you let those enter who are trying to.'

William had made the first tentative steps towards seeking God's Kingdom but the door had been temporarily shut in his face. He had no understanding of the treasures that lay behind the façade of false religion. He stood confused and alone, waiting at the entrance to the Kingdom for someone to show him the way to a life of eternity.

For three daunting years, he continued earnestly to seek. He never gave up searching until he received an answer to his questions in the form of Jesus Christ, His Saviour. On that day, God revealed to him that it is all about relationship and not religion. William recognised that he had been accepted into God's family.

As a boy, he had lost his dad but now he had a child / father bond with the Lord Almighty. He also now had an older brother called Jesus. He was a brother, like no other who had made the ultimate sacrifice to make a way back to God when there was no other way. There was more – he had also been given a gentle companion and helper to walk alongside him. The Holy Spirit was to be his advisor: to teach, prompt, reveal and guide throughout his earthly years.

William had been anticipating this moment for years. He took the revelation with all its promises and possibilities and ran with it. He was not going to waste any more precious time. He was a newborn at the beginning of an exciting venture into a new life. He began to listen to others who had trod this road before him. They encouraged him to go deeper in his new-found relationship. He responded by diving down into the word, praying and listening, with an awareness that this was going to be a lifelong pursuit.

William found joy in the realisation that His God wanted to be close up and personal. He was not like a distant benevolent uncle that turned up on high days and holidays. He was family in the strongest and purest sense, tied together by the blood of Jesus. It was a day of celebrations in the Heavens and in William's heart when he left religion behind and swapped it for a beautiful, ever-lasting, relationship with a living God.

Our first legacy lesson is to understand and accept that the God of all creation wants to adopt each and every one of us. He is waiting to embrace us into a new beginning with Him so we can call ourselves children of God. All of us who belong to Him are sons and daughters of the King. We are fully established in the royal household, we are relational, we have come home and we are family. It's time to leave behind any form or fragment of false religion and fully immerse ourselves in a rich and rewarding relationship with God the Father, God the Son and God the Holy Spirit.

Legacy Lesson Two
The Gift of Grace

There for the grace of God go I: a popular idiom, spoken out by an on-looker when someone finds themselves in difficult circumstances. *A fall from grace* is a phrase often used about a public figure referring to a loss of status and respect because of some misdemeanour. They only had 'one *saving grace*' speaks of a person's only good quality among a number of character shortcomings. *Grace* is the word regularly used to clarify and pacify awkward situations: but what does it actually mean?

The word grace has been in use for centuries and has many different meanings in the English language including elegance, virtue, mercy, a short prayer or a formal title. It can be used in many situations but for followers of Jesus it is a special, profound word full of love and assurance and is integral to the Christian faith. It is an everyday, extraordinary expression that encompasses and expounds the fulfilment of God's promise of salvation.

Until he was in his early twenties, William knew nothing about the grace of God. He believed in a higher being but had no knowledge of the perfect plan that promised him a life of liberty. He strived for his own perfection, believing that a ticket to Heaven relied on his own strength and moral willpower. He failed at every turn becoming downcast and dejected until the day his life changed forever.

After an invite from his brother, William travelled to a local town to listen to a sermon spoken by an itinerant preacher. The sermon turned out to be like no other sermon he had ever heard before. An ordinary man, empowered by the love of God, stood before him and the crowd that had gathered, speaking passionately about the redeeming, restorative power of Christ's blood that had been shed on a cross at Calvary, outside the walls of Jerusalem. No one had ever talked to him in such terms before and for William it was a moment of revelation.

He realised that the sin in the world had created an enormous divide between The Creator and His people and that the only way for that divide to be bridged was through an atoning sacrifice. So for the sake of man and womankind God sent His Only Son to live on Earth before being crucified in the cruellest way on a Roman cross. Three days later Jesus miraculously rose again, defeating sin and gaining victory over death. Jesus paid the ultimate price so that eternal life was available for all.

As William heard the words of the preacher and they settled in his heart, he received a deep understanding of the sacrifice Jesus had freely undergone. This was God's grace: a gift that was lovingly given to an undeserving people to restore the relationship between God and the inhabitants of Earth. He now knew, in his heart, that through grace, God had made a way for him to be saved.

Ephesians 2:8-10:

> For it is by grace you have been saved, through faith - and this is not from yourselves, it is the gift of God, not by works, so that no one can boast. For we are God's handiwork, created in Christ Jesus to do good works, which God prepared in advance for us to do.

All that was required from William was to acknowledge his part as a sinner, repent, ask for forgiveness, accept His gift and believe. No amount of good works or moral upright behaviour could save him. The solution was Jesus and armed with this revelation, he accepted Jesus fully into his life, knowing that the only way to God was through Him. William was no longer bound by sin. He knew he had been forgiven and given eternal life. Jesus had done it all. It was a free gift from God.

As a born again believer, he lost no time in grasping the richness of his salvation. He progressed rapidly from having no comprehension of grace; believing salvation was in his own hands, to knowing the power of freedom in Christ. It was an instantaneous transformation. The door had been opened and he had walked in, with the confidence that he knew who he was in Christ.

From that moment on, he was desperate to feed on the word of God, eager to discover and discern all the truths and treasures in the pages of the Bible. By regularly reading Scriptures and praying, he created a solid foundation for his faith. His mind-set altered as his obedience and commitment to Christ took root and quickly grew.

Despite his new found enthusiasm and deepening conviction, he still found himself occasionally on a meandering road. He had doubts and insecurities rise up, reminding him of who he used to be. On one particular occasion, he read the Bible and tried to pray but was so weighed down by the way he felt about the sin in his life that he was unable to utter a word. He had put himself back in condemnation again but he did not stay there. It took him a day of anguish to work it through, once more coming to the conclusion that he was covered by grace and could do nothing to redeem himself apart from accepting the gift that Christ had given him. God's word told him that he was free so who was he to self-judge and criticise?

Romans 8:1:

> Therefore, there is now no condemnation for those who are in Christ Jesus, because through Christ Jesus the law of the Spirit who gives life has set you free from the law of sin and death.

It was time for William to resolve to fully accept and live in the amazing grace that Christ bought for him with the shedding of His blood. It is the most precious gift that we can ever be given and it comes not only with a promise of freedom but also of a full life.

In John 10:10 Jesus says:

> ...I have come that they may have life, and have it to the full.

William wanted to live his life to the full with Jesus.

Our second legacy lesson is that the grace given to William is a, no strings attached, gift for everyone that believes in Jesus Christ and receives Him as Lord and Saviour. Titus 2:11 says

> For the grace of God has appeared that offers salvation to all people.

God wants everyone to accept His grace so that we can all be in a fulfilling relationship with Him: a spiritual bond that will last for eternity. Grace is a combination of God's Redeeming Action and Christ's Endowment.

As part of this lesson, we need to understand that Jesus not only died to give us eternal life, He also made the sacrifice to take away all our anxieties and worries so we can live complete lives. He has broken the chains that bind us, and has made a way for us to live in gracious liberty. Grace is the free, unmerited favour of God. It not only calls us and saves us it sustains us spiritually and emotionally and will follow us to eternity. It is the gift that keeps on giving.

Legacy Lesson Three
Milk or Maturity?

Some things are better served mature and these include cheese, wine and Christians. Alas, for followers of Christ aging is not synonymous with maturity. Ninety-year-olds can be babes in Christ, while young people can display spiritual discernment and insight. Unlike a bottle of port believers do not automatically get better (sweeter, more mellow) with age. Wrinkles do not always embody wisdom and salvation is not a declaration of maturity.

We are called to be spiritually mature: but what does it mean? Is it obedience, moral excellence, scriptural knowledge, a particular mind-set or an attitude of heart? The answer is to be found in the perfect example of Christ. He is our standard and mature growth starts with us being united with Him. He is the vine feeding its branches so they grow, fully develop and bear much fruit. Jesus is the key to spiritual progress.

When William experienced the extraordinary miracle of salvation, he became wondrously united with Jesus. It was a pivotal moment, the beginning of a redemptive, eternal relationship. The initial euphoria he felt filled him with guileless enthusiasm, with no concept of the steps he would subsequently take to become mature in Christ. Having been delivered from the sins that had tied him in knots, he was basking in the revelation of grace and eternal life. Consequently, and completely justifiably, he was still young in his spiritual reflection, rationale and reasoning. It was a time of celebration, a time of and joy and anticipation to be savoured and cherished before advancing onwards in his Christian walk.

Hebrews 6:1:

> Therefore, let us move beyond the elementary teachings about Christ and be taken forward to maturity...

It is an encouragement to move on from spiritual infancy. Having understood and delighted in the basics of faith and repentance, it is now imperative to dig deeper and discover more of God's treasures.

William's understanding was still that of a child but eager to learn, he took every opportunity to hear God's word.

It was a cold winter's morning when he discovered the importance of being mature in Christ. Sat on a straw bale, in a friend's barn, listening to a fellow Christian preach on a passage originally written for God's holy people in Colossae.

Colossians 1:28:

> He is the one we proclaim, admonishing and teaching everyone with all wisdom, so that we may present everyone fully mature in Christ.

It was a timely message. William already had *an old head on young shoulders*, giving out an air of responsibility and reliability, but this was a different kind of maturity. This was to do with spiritual experience and growth and the actions necessary to fully mature in Christ: to be all that God fully intended him to be.

Up to this point, William had been drinking spiritual milk; the perfect nourishment for a time, satisfying his needs just like those of a newborn baby. The milk had laid down a strong foundation for further growth but now he needed to progress to solid food so he could fully develop. Without it, at best, he would remain like a child and, at worst, he would spiritually fade and wither away.

As William listened to the sermon, he took the words to heart; he internalised the message, thought about it seriously and began trying to live up to the teachings he had heard.

Most people do not appreciate being criticised or rebuked. When children are chastised for their own good, they can choose to either disregard or accept the advice given. In the same way, William at this juncture had a choice to be rebellious or obedient. He chose the latter and settled his mind to act on biblical principles as he journeyed towards *adulthood*.

His first step was to prepare himself to be able to recognise and accept loving admonishment from people wiser than he was. He needed to acknowledge that he could learn a lot from those with more know-how and insight. Secondly, he needed to appreciate the need and benefits of listening to wise biblical teaching. It was going to be easier for him to grow up with the help of others - to learn the lessons that they had once been taught.

As a tailor if he had tried to sew together a garment without training or practical example it would have, inevitably, gone wrong, ending up ill-fitting and not suitable for purpose. The same applied to the task he was now embarking upon. William needed sound instruction and teaching from those who were more mature to help him develop a solid spiritual life that would equip him for the future that God had planned for him.

There is also a caution that goes along with this.

1 Corinthians: 3:2:

> Brothers and sisters, I could not address you as people who live by the Spirit but as people who are still worldly—mere infants in Christ. I gave you milk, not solid food, for you were not yet ready for it. Indeed, you are still not ready.

Paul was speaking to the members of a young church who had not yet reached a state of maturity. He had built the foundation for them when he founded the church in Corinth and now others were building on it. Unfortunately, division, had reared its head, creating jealousy among them. Some people followed Paul, while others followed Apollos (a converted Jew who spoke with eloquence). Paul's caution to them was to base their faith on the foundation stone of Jesus Christ and not to follow or venerate those who speak out the Good News.

Being in a Christ centred environment and mixing with Christ focused people is the perfect place to flourish and progress. It is a template laid down by Jesus Himself, to train and prepare His disciples.

Ephesians 4:11-13:

> So Christ Himself gave the apostles, the prophets, the evangelists, the pastors and teachers, to equip His people for works of service, so that the body of Christ may be built up until we all reach unity in the faith and in the knowledge of the Son of God and become mature, attaining to the whole measure of the fullness of Christ. Then we will no longer be infants, tossed back and forth by the waves, and blown here and there by every wind of teaching and by the cunning and craftiness of people in their deceitful scheming.

Throughout his life, William worked towards what he referred to as *spiritual advancement*. He read the word, prayed and asked God to reveal profound truths to him. When he had challenges, he dealt with them in a considered and sensible way, reflecting the person he had become. When he was persecuted because of his faith, he never reacted in kind. He chose to use the negative trials to test and refine his character. William did not allow himself to be side-tracked, either by the cares of his day or by the common escapisms of nineteenth century pastimes. He clearly saw the transient nature of his earthly life and the opposing, eternal quality of God's Kingdom.

Understanding and applying our third legacy lesson is crucial, if we are to be transformed and not remain spiritually needy babies. We need a desire to go beyond conversion and into discipleship. Growing in maturity in Christ is open to all, not just leaders, vicars, committee members or Sunday School teachers. Everyone who has a relationship with Christ is called to be fully developed in Him.

If we are to change, grow and develop, we must put aside vain, temporary distractions and focus our minds on Christ. God has so much more in store for us beyond our salvation. He knows our potential and wants us to be fulfilled.

In light of this, we have to ask ourselves the question; do we want to drink milk for the rest of our days, or do we want to grow up? Do we want to stay in infanthood or grow to be presented as mature disciples in Christ? It is a decision. The choice is ours. The choice is yours.

Legacy Lesson Four
Prayer, Privilege and Power

Prayer is a privilege. Prayer is a powerful spiritual communion with God. Prayer is a two-way communication between Heaven and Earth. The Creator of the universe has designed a way to interact with people on a profoundly personal level: for individuals to speak to Him in confidence, thankfulness and joy. He listens and wants to be heard. God wants His children to recognise when He is speaking, just as sheep learn to identify and trust the guiding sound of the shepherd's voice.

The sad reality for some Christians is that prayer is not a popular or prevalent pastime unless there is an urgent need to be met. It can be seen as a bore or a chore, a duty instead of a delightful dialogue. The truth is prayer should be a priority, both in good times and bad and not used as a tool for potential personal gain. It is a supernatural God-given way to build a deep, trusting relationship with our Heavenly Father and it should be treated with respect and reverence.

William turned to God for the first time in prayer because he was afraid. He was fearful for the future of his family. He had no real idea who God was but something in his spirit drew him to cry out to a Being beyond himself. He and his kin were desperately hungry, almost destitute and deprived of any earthly comforts. It was a hopeless situation until William prayed, requesting help. He asked God to give him work, to help him succeed in his labours to bring his household back from the brink of homelessness and starvation. His request did not come from a selfish motive for money but from a desire and compassion for the ones, he loved. It was a simple heartfelt prayer and the beginning of a lifetime's trust and reliance on an amazing God who listens and answers.

In a childlike response to a physical need, William discovered prayer. God heard him and in His infinite mercy, responded, reaching down to touch the heart of a lost boy. As an adult, William came to understand the power and privilege of prayer and chose to make it a priority in his life.

Early on in his ministry, he recognised the importance of daily prayer. He established the habit of getting up in the morning to spend time alone, read the word and pray.

Mathew 6:6:

> But when you pray, go into your room, close the door and pray to your Father, who is unseen. Then your Father, who sees what is done in secret, will reward you.

Despite the crowded, cramped conditions that he lived in, he managed to find a small spot where he could be alone with the Lord, a precious place of prayer. It was also his custom to finish the day conversing with God; thanking Him for all his goodness and provision throughout the day. Praying was his first act upon waking up and his final action before sleep.

William's world was a place of great need and some days he became *anxious for the want of food*. It was a very natural response but it never took him long to realign his thoughts and prayers to the words of Scripture. On one occasion, when he was tired and faint from hunger, William prayed to the Lord to help him, to give him strength to cope with his situation. No sooner had he prayed than his mind grew more composed and he became still, trusting in a faithful God. He was still hungry but his spiritual strength was renewed and subsequently food was provided for him. William had an absolute belief that God would always supply his needs. He knew that prayer can dispel anxiety and bring a pure peace of mind to a troubled soul.

Philippians: 4:6-7:

> Do not be anxious about anything, but in every situation, by prayer and petition, with thanksgiving, present your requests to God. And the peace of God, which transcends all understanding, will guard your hearts and your minds in Christ Jesus.

Motive matters when it comes to prayer. Without spiritual unity and intimacy in Christ, prayers can be self-centred and not God focussed. William quickly learnt this secret to answered prayer. When he prayed, he asked God to reveal spiritual things to him, the deeper truths and meanings of His word. He did not ask for material wealth or secular success. He spent time petitioning on behalf of the lost and seeking the Kingdom of God.

James 4:3:

> When you ask, you do not receive, because you ask with wrong motives, that you may spend what you get on your pleasures.

When he was twenty-three, he initiated a prayer group with two friends, specifically to pray for the spiritual state of his village. They prayed secretly every week for several months before they began to see the fruits of their faithfulness. Throughout this time, William was learning to be patient while waiting for a perfectly timed response from God. The answer to their supplications came slowly and gently. It was more like a refreshing breeze than a rush of wind as the prayers of the three men paved the way for a fresh Spirit-breathed coming of God's love and purpose, blowing away the shadows and making way for the light.

William and his friend's prayers were being answered, not because they were special or because they had a good idea but because they were in Christ. They were in union and communion with Jesus and, because of this, their prayers and wishes were in alignment with the will of God and His future plans.

John 15:7-8:

> If you remain in me and my words remain in you, ask whatever you wish, and it will be done for you. This is to my Father's glory, that you bear much fruit, showing yourselves to be my disciples.

1 John 5:14-15:

> This is the confidence we have in approaching God: that if we ask anything according to His will, He hears us. And if we know that He hears us-whatever we ask-we know that we have what we asked of Him.

Jesus is our greatest example when it comes to making prayer a high priority. He is both the Son of God and fully God.

John 10:30:

> I and the Father are one.

They are uniquely connected and in perfect spiritual union with one another, yet Jesus still took time out to have Heavenly fellowship with His Father. He often went away to a quiet place to pray alone, spending hours in communion together.

Luke 6:12:

> One of those days, Jesus went out to a mountainside to pray, and spent the night praying to God.

Before His death Jesus prayed on the Mount of Olives saying,

> Father, if you are willing, take this cup from me; yet not my will, but yours be done.

He knew the path that lay ahead of him and despite His misgivings in that moment, he still yielded to the will of His Father.

Our plea should always be 'Not my will, God but yours.' He knows what is best for us. We need to put away our own agendas. He does not need our prompts and plans. Pray for God's ideas not good ideas.

Our fourth legacy lesson is to always remain in Christ and make prayer a powerful priority in our lives. We should be patient and pray for God's will to be done in every situation as we line up our desires with His. Prayer is free. There are no call charges! Jesus made a way for us all to approach our Heavenly Father in total liberty. Wherever we are in our journey He wants us to talk to Him and enjoy the deep joy and fulfilment that communing with God brings.

Prayer – Prioritise, Relate, Ask, Yield, Expect, Receive.

Legacy Lesson Five
Money Matters

Money is the root of all evil, is probably high up on the list of misquotes from the Bible. The truth is, money is not evil but the love of it is. Mind-set is what matters.

1 Timothy 6:10:

> For the love of money is a root of all kinds of evil. Some people, eager for money, have wandered from the faith and pierced themselves with many griefs.

Money always has the potential to be a contentious subject between individuals, within families and in business. The desire for it causes arguments, division, jealousy, pride, greed, temptation and crime. It has the ability to destroy lives but also, with the right attitude and in the right hands, has the potential to be a tool for good.

Matthew 6:24:

> No one can serve two masters. Either you will hate the one and love the other, or you will be devoted to the one and despise the other. You cannot serve both God and money.

William served God and his relationship with money was inconsequential. It was a necessity but never a desire. He never chased after wealth, despite living with dire finances for many years. In his own words, when he was a child, his family were left in *a condition of great destitution*. This was poverty so extreme that they lacked the means to provide for themselves. They were often *distressed for lack of food*. William really knew what it was like to be without the basics needed to survive but instead of complaining, his response was to pray. He prayed, not for money, but for enough work so he could meet their needs.

He knew what it was to be penniless and hungry, to feel the gnawing pain in the pit of his stomach. When there was little or no food on the table, he did not go out to beg, borrow or steal instead he prayed for God to *give him strength equal to the day*. When he felt faint and weary for lack of food, he trusted that the Lord would provide and he was never disappointed. William was taken to the *wire* on many occasions but his faith was always rewarded. He believed in God's bountiful provision and was always grateful for everything he had.

Many people in his situation would have vowed never to be poor again and gone out into the world to make their fortune – a rags to riches story that authors love to write about. Instead, William chose to put no value on material wealth. He never knew what it was like to be rich and he never craved money but that did not deter him from loving God, with all his heart, and relying on Him for all provision.

When he gave a statement on providence at the opening of the Long Crendon Baptist church, he acknowledged that everything came from God and he continued in that belief regardless of his circumstances.

Romans 11:36:

> For from Him and through Him and for Him are all things.
> To Him be the glory forever! Amen.

Psalm 24:1:

> The Earth is the Lord's, and everything in it, the world, and all who live in it.

William held a different perspective to the view of the world and saw poverty as a temporal thing; an earthly condition that had far less importance when compared to spiritual hunger. He was motivated by the wealth found in heavenly riches. He knew where real value lay.

In the early days of writing his diary, he wrote:

I saw this evening that nothing could give me any satisfaction in this world; my mind seemed weaned from all earthly objects; I could delight but in one thing – to be doing something for Jesus Christ.

Mathew 6:19:

> Do not store up for yourselves treasures on Earth, where moths and vermin destroy, and where thieves break in and steal. But store up for yourselves treasures in Heaven, where moths and vermin do not destroy, and where thieves do not break in and steal. For where your treasure is, there your heart will be also.

William was content with his lot. He did not strive to have a cupboard full of food, a wardrobe of smart clothes, the latest carriage or a bigger, better house. He took the good times and the bad in his stride, knowing that he was in God's hands. The next two passages sum up William's attitude perfectly.

Philippians 4:19:

> And my God will meet all your needs according to the riches of His glory in Christ Jesus.

1 Timothy 6:6-8:

> But godliness with contentment is great gain. For we brought nothing into the world, and we can take nothing out of it. But if we have food and clothing, we will be content with that.

As followers of Jesus, God is always at work in our circumstances, whether we are rich or poor. Our task is to seek the Kingdom of God, and the rest will fall into place. It is important to realise spiritual blessing does not equate with material wealth. God in His infinite wisdom chooses the best for His children.

1 Samuel 2:7:

> The Lord sends poverty and wealth; He humbles and He exalts.

It is a difficult concept to grasp, particularly in a materialistic society but being rich is not better than being poor. Wealth is fleeting and of no relevance to our eternal lives. It can give us a life of comfort but that in itself can make it more difficult to assume total reliance on God.

1 Timothy 6:17:

> Command those who are rich in this present world not to be arrogant nor to put their hope in wealth, which is so uncertain, but to put their hope in God, who richly provides us with everything for our enjoyment.

For those of us who have been blessed with more than enough then we should use our excess wisely. We should be good stewards of the money

God has entrusted to us. It is not the state of our finances that is in question; it is the condition of our heart and the leaning of our attitude.

It is not only the wealthy who need to take note. We can be less than solvent and spend all our waking thoughts dreaming about winning the lottery or hatching *get rich quick* schemes. Money should never be an end in itself. Our eyes need to be lifted beyond the fortunes of this world to gaze firmly on the riches to be discovered in the Kingdom of God.

Matthew 6:21:

> For where your treasure is, there your heart will be also.

This is our next legacy lesson. A healthy, Bible-based attitude to money and material possessions, to acknowledge who is responsible for everything we have in life. To be satisfied. If we are content with what we have then we have everything. Think about it! Our most treasured possessions will one day be dust, rust or lying stagnant in a landfill. Everything we believe we own is a transient gift. *We can't take it with us when we die*, might be a cliché but it's a true one.

Think about it. The only thing on this Earth that will remain forever is the word of God. Ask yourself is money your motivator? Is it your master? Where do you put your trust and security? Is your heart on Earth or is it in Heaven? Where do you keep your treasures? Think about it!

Legacy Lesson Six
Working Well

Work is an activity that can conjure up delight in some and dread in others. It can be fulfilling or fruitless, bracing or boring, paid or not paid. It involves mental or physical effort in order to achieve an end goal. The Beatles and Dolly Parton have famously sung about it and countless poems have been penned extolling its virtues or lamenting its woes.

Whether it is loved or loathed, work is part of the human experience. For some people, it defines them as they labour to accomplish their *life's work*. Others use it as a means to an end to reap the rewards of their toil in monetary terms. Regardless of why people work, it is a major cog in the wheels of society that keeps on turning from generation to generation.

In the early part of the nineteenth century, children from poor families had to grow up working. They did not have the luxury of a cherished childhood or the privilege of school. Every penny counted and even though they were young, they were expected to contribute to the coffers. William was no exception. As soon as he was capable of running an errand or performing some menial task, he was given an occupation. Working was not an option it was a necessity.

As a young man, William came to understand the demands of responsibility and the expectations that such knowledge placed upon him. He worked hard to further his prospects in his desire to make enough money to feed clothe and home his family. Remarkably, once he had made *enough*, he chose to spend his spare time on more spiritual pursuits. He could have easily used every waking hour to create more income but he recognised that excessive material wealth was a short-lived distraction and he had no craving to chase it. He made an active decision to seek God and not gold.

John 6:27:

> Do not work for food that spoils, but for food that endures to eternal life, which the Son of Man will give you. For on Him God the Father has placed His seal of approval.

Within this balance of working for a living and seeking God's kingdom, he understood his obligation to provide and tried hard not to shirk his duty. In the early 19th century, there were few benefit buffers. If he did not work, he and his family faced eviction and life out on the streets, at the mercy of meagre outdoor relief (basic social welfare for the homeless). He was following biblical teaching.

1 Timothy 5:8:

> Anyone who does not provide for their relatives, and especially for their own household, has denied the faith and is worse than an unbeliever.

He was blessed to be physically and mentally able to work but there were many obstacles for him to overcome to earn a living. He never gave up. He lacked education so he taught himself; he had no transport so he walked; the locals turned against him so he went further afield to get business. He was a determined man.

William's desire to work came from an aspiration to better himself so he could do God's work. In everything he did, he became the best he could be because he was working for the Kingdom. For William, being engaged in the Lord's work was where his heart was. His efforts were for an eternal purpose.

Colossians 3:23:

> Whatever you do, work at it with all your heart, as working for the Lord, not for human masters.

He acknowledged that his work in any capacity needed to be blessed by God. William spent considerable time in prayer, concerning his future and his small part in God's bigger picture; praying for God's will in his life.

Proverbs 16:3:

> Commit to the Lord whatever you do, and He will establish your plans.

William was a conscientious worker and as a minister gave his all, putting others needs before his own. He did not expect his congregation to provide fully for him. Instead, he raised funds by continuing to practise tailoring, while still spreading the Gospel and taking care of the spiritual needs of others. Like the apostle Paul, who used his skill as a tent maker to earn his keep, William paid his own way and did not look to others to support him.

Acts 20:33-34:

> I have not coveted anyone's silver or gold or clothing. You yourselves know that these hands of mine have supplied my own needs and the needs of my companions.

The antithesis of hard work is laziness. The book of proverbs has numerous comments on the consequences of an idle lifestyle, for those capable of work. It does not sugar coat its statements. The word sluggard is used repeatedly to describe a habitually lazy person.

Proverbs 20:4:

> Sluggards do not plough in season; so at harvest time they look but find nothing.

This is an analogy with a far deeper meaning than the harvesting of food from a field. There is a season to work and for the sluggard there are consequences to being idle. The effects of laziness are not always immediately evident but one day, there will come a harvest day. Perpetual idleness will result in spiritual and mental futility and emptiness.

Proverbs 21:25:

> The craving of a sluggard will be the death of him, because his hands refuse to work.

Wanting without working is a dangerous game to play. The yearning for things beyond reach creates feelings of jealousy, bitterness self-pity, melancholy and hate. It is a breeding ground for spiritual apathy and death.

Proverbs 6:6:

> Go to the ant, you sluggard; consider its ways and be wise!

After the slating of the sluggard, comes solution. Look at the ant. It is fascinating to watch these busy little creatures. They are fast, running around in an apparently haphazard fashion when in fact they are efficient and organised. They are practical and productive, smart, strong and skilled. They communicate and cooperate, working independently and as a team. Ants are a perfect example of a good work ethic. Be more ant!

It is clear that God intended us to work diligently but He also directs us to rest and recuperate. When God created the world, He took six days and on the seventh, He rested. It was included in the Sabbath laws that Moses related to the Israelites on God's instructions.

Exodus 23:12:

> Six days do your work, but on the seventh day do not work...

This law may have applied to the Jews and comes from the old covenant before the sacrifice of Jesus, but it is still good advice. Taking a day off once a week is beneficial to both mental and physical health. More importantly, it is about trusting God and relying fully on Him to be able to relax.

Jesus is the true rest for our souls and William understood both the importance of working for God and of resting in Him. God does not need to command us religiously to take a day off because Jesus came to give us real rest.

Mathew 11:28-30:

> Come to me, all you who are weary and burdened, and I will give you rest. Take my yoke upon you and learn from me, for I am gentle and humble in heart, and you will find rest for your souls. For my yoke is easy and my burden is light.

Our sixth legacy lesson should be a challenge for most of us. Are we sluggards for self or servants for God? When it comes to work, God knows our personal limitations. Some people in society are not able to work so for those folks there is no need for self-condemnation or protestations. For the rest of us, who and what are we working for? Are we working as if for the Lord with all our heart?

No matter how boring or exciting our task in hand, if we do it for the Lord then it changes our perspective. Love and integrity become embedded in our work ethic as we serve God and not our own satisfaction or ego. He is not a hard taskmaster and wants us to burn from within with the passion found in Christ and not burn out from over work.

If you love Jesus, then use your gifts and talents and put your hands, feet and mind, not just to good use but to God's use.

Legacy Lesson Seven
Guard the Gospel

Society guards its most precious items. Fort Knox gold depository in the USA is one of the most heavily guarded and secure places in the world. In the UK, the crown jewels, held in trust by the king for the nation, are kept under armed guard in the Tower of London. The perceived worth of the items is in direct correlation to the allotted level of protection.

The people selected to ensure the security of the treasures are vetted, in part, for their honesty, integrity and vigilance. The safeguarding of a nation's most prized possessions is entrusted into the care of those most capable of succeeding in the job.

Gold and precious gems may be costly but they count as nothing when compared to the *pricelessness* of the Gospel of God. Despite its value, it is not hidden away in a vault, instead, God liberates it, entrusting its guardianship into the hands of those who love Him. It is a responsible job but one that they have been prepared and provided for. He takes the followers of Jesus and puts into their hands a task for which they are well equipped.

When William first became a minister, he was given the following words:

1 Timothy 6:20-21:

> Timothy, guard what has been entrusted to your care. Turn away from godless chatter and the opposing ideas of what is falsely called knowledge, which some have professed and in so doing have departed from the faith. Grace be with you all.

This personal message was being directly addressed to William.

He was being urged to guard what God had entrusted to him. To protect the Gospel: the legitimacy of God's word. The truth was not to be compromised. William's duty was to watch over it, to shield it and defend it from damage or derision. He was respected, as a man and a follower of Christ. The elders knew that they could trust him with the task in hand. They recognised in him a person who was faithful and reliable, someone who could be depended upon.

He was reminded to avoid godless, foolish discussions with those who believed themselves to be knowledgeable and those that wanted to pick a verbal fight. Arguments of this type are a waste of precious time, drawing people into dangerous distractions.

William took the words that had been written to Timothy, and diligently applied them to his own situation as he took on his first ministerial role. It was nearly two thousand years since Paul's words had been penned but there were still people in William's vicinity who wanted to dilute the truth, with an agenda to weaken the word of God.

Throughout his life, William came up against individuals who made it a personal challenge to try to chip away at the truth of the Gospel, often with a desire to replace it with law and sanctimonious religion but he always stood strong and held his ground. He was steadfast in the face of lies. He stood up for what he believed in, defending his faith with maturity and intelligence.

How did William effectively guard the Gospel? How do Christians in the 21st century effectively guard the Gospel? The only way is through obedience with the power and guidance of the Holy Spirit as He leads us into truth. It is not going to be a party in the park. It is going to be a blood red battle.

There is an enemy out there and he wants to blur the lines between black and white, into a subtle, grim-reaper grey. Pray for discernment and keep in mind the following words that Jesus said to His disciples.

Matthew 10:16:

> I am sending you out like sheep among wolves. Therefore, be as shrewd as snakes and as innocent as doves.

The world is full of pit-falls and traps waiting to trip up the unsuspecting. Jesus' instruction is to be wise in avoiding such snares; to be able to understand and judge risky situations and scenarios quickly. He also encourages His disciples to be innocent, to be pure in heart without being gullible or naive.

It is a spiritual battle and we are directed to put on the armour of God to be able to stand and fight.

Ephesians 6:14-17:

> Stand firm then, with the belt of truth buckled around your waist, with the breastplate of righteousness in place, and with your feet fitted with the readiness that comes from the gospel of peace. In addition to all this, take up the shield of faith, with which you can extinguish all the flaming arrows of the evil one. Take the helmet of salvation and the sword of the Spirit, which is the word of God.

The next step is discipline against distraction. The root word of discipline is disciple, which means someone who studies. In essence a student who receives training and instruction, applying to their lives the things they have learnt. Spend time in the word of God, allowing the Spirit to teach and empower. The application of Scripture will help protect against distraction.

Proverbs 4:25-27:

> Let your eyes look straight ahead; fix your gaze directly before you. Give careful thought to the paths for your feet

> and be steadfast in all your ways. Do not turn to the right or the left; keep your foot from evil.

Read, inwardly digest and understand the precious truths that God has revealed through His Son and the saving grace of the Gospel. Then go out and share with others everything that has been received. Reveal the treasures of Scripture with sound interpretation and live according to its truths.

2 Timothy 2:15:

> Do your best to present yourself to God as one approved, a worker who does not need to be ashamed and who correctly handles the word of truth.

There is also a warning not to get involved in senseless, hypothetical or academic disagreements with people who want to argue for the sake of it. God's truth is not negotiable. When Jesus was preaching His sermon on the mount, He gave a warning, to protect the honour of the Gospel.

Matthew 7:6:

> Do not give dogs what is sacred; do not throw your pearls to pigs. If you do, they may trample them under their feet, and turn and tear you to pieces.

Jesus used this analogy to alert disciples to the problem of relating the Good News to people who are known to ridicule and reject the word of God. If you give a dog something holy, he will take it in his mouth and rip it apart with no knowledge of its significance. Likewise, if you throw precious pearls to a pig they will have no use for them and trample them underfoot. If the Gospel is not welcome, move on. Do not give anyone the opportunity to mock God's word.

Our penultimate legacy lesson teaches us that we should all safeguard what God has entrusted to us, not just those with a degree in theology or a paid position in the church. If we love Jesus, then it is our responsibility to defend the faith. Learn to discern, to differentiate between a fertile area and a barren place. Walk away from those who come against the authenticity of the Bible with foolish talk and lies without legs. Take care not to allow His pure truth to be corrupted, contaminated, or diluted.

Know the truth with your entire mind. Believe it with all your heart. Live it with all your passion. Protect it with all your might.

The God of all creation has trusted you with something very precious to Him - the Gospel. Guard it well.

Legacy Lesson Eight
Heart or Hand?

This final legacy lesson is a personal message from me to you. It is a lifetime lesson that has been honed through countless mistakes and misunderstandings. It is a continuing lesson that renews itself daily because I still have much to learn.

Do you want a full and mature relationship with God the Father God the Son and God the Holy Spirit?
Do you want to live fully in the grace that Jesus gifted you?
Do you want to be focussed on prayer and not on money?
Do you want to be entrusted to work well and guard the Gospel?

If the answer is YES and you are serious then determine to:
Seek His manna and not His money.
Seek His presence and not His presents.
Seek His heart and not His hand.
Seek His face and not His favour.

Four different statements with the same core meaning. All of them designed to challenge your understanding of God's relational role in your life.

When the Jews were stranded in the wilderness for forty years, they were sent manna from Heaven to eat. It sustained them and kept them from death. Without Jesus, the world was a desert; parched from lack of living water and so He came down to Earth to be *manna*; to be the Bread of Life: to restore the sin-shattered relationship between God and mankind. There is only one way to God and that is through Jesus. You need manna not money. Seek first the kingdom of God and the Lord, Jehovah Jireh always has and will always provide.

Mathew 6:31-32:

> So do not worry, saying, 'What shall we eat?' or 'What shall we drink?' or 'What shall we wear?' For the pagans run after all these things, and your Heavenly Father knows that you need them. But seek first His kingdom and His righteousness, and all these things will be given to you as well.

God is not a three-wish, out of the bottle genie. He is not an on-line convenience shop. He is not a philanthropic business executive to be swayed by great ideas. God can and does bless you with many things but that is not His ultimate aspiration. If all He ever is to you is a bountiful benefactor supplying your needs and wants, then you have failed to understand the rich rapport that God offers. What He desires most is a relationship with you based on reciprocal love. He wants you to love Him for who He is and not what He can give you. He wants you to seek Him out, to pursue and search Him out by any method.

Jeremiah 29:12-14:

> Then you will call on me and come and pray to me, and I will listen to you. You will seek me and find me when you seek me with all your heart. I will be found by you,' declares the Lord, 'and will bring you back from captivity.

These were God's words to the Israelites when they were in exile in Babylon but they still have a deep relevant meaning. Seek His heart with all your heart and you will find Him. He wants to be revealed. Find Him and be free of anything that holds you captive.

God constantly invites you to seek Him; to seek His presence but more than that, He asks that you seek His face. Seeking God's beautiful face is synonymous with seeking His presence but it indicates a more intimate connection. He is not offering a superficial once in a lifetime glimpse of a supreme, un-relatable being. God is giving an opportunity for you to have an ongoing, profound, up close and personal relationship with someone whose love for you knows no bounds.

1 Chronicles 16:11:

> Look to the Lord and His strength; seek His face always.

Getting to know your Creator is exciting! He longs for you to be close to Him. Pray, worship and read His word with the purpose of knowing Him. Find new ways to seek Him out. The bond between you is unique so be bespoke in honouring and celebrating the love you share! Delight in Him. Write Him a love letter. Pen a psalm of praise. Sing a new song! Seek His heart and His face and be blessed.

Epilogue

I never knew William personally but his writings and his life have guided, uplifted and inspired me. The lessons are real and relevant. He understood the legacy that God's adopted children have been entrusted with. He recognised our responsibility to pass it on. He realised the importance of writing our journey down so that future generations know where they have come from.

Finding out that William Hopcraft shared the same faith as me was such a beautiful revelation in my life. I thank God for William and I thank God for revealing my spiritual inheritance.

My job here is now done. This is my legacy left for my children, grandchildren and future generations. My prayer is that to the reader of this book it will make a difference. May you continue the legacy by living and breathing the lessons within.

I leave the right destination of these words in the hands of the Almighty. It might be tomorrow, next month, next year, next decade or in two hundred years… all in God's time.

I give all the credit to Jesus. He is the author of my life; the author of my salvation and the author and finisher of my faith.

Bibliography

Aylesbury News, 31st December 1836

Baptist Magazine April 1811, February 1816, June 1822, July 1830

Baptist Records, Long Crendon Baptist Church

Bucks Advertiser and Aylesbury News, February 1839

Census Records, Buckinghamshire Records Office

Northampton Mercury March 1829

Notes on a Decayed Needle-land. Compiled by William Shrimpton. Reprinted from The Redditch Indicator, 1897

On Caring for The Souls of Others, The Circular Letter from the Ministers and Messengers of the Buckinghamshire Association of Baptist Churches Assembled at Long Crendon, May 11th & 12th 1841

Oxford Journal, March 1822

Oxford University and City Herald, January 1825

St Mary's Parish Records, Buckinghamshire Records Office

The History of the Long Crendon Baptist Church and Sunday School. Compiled by S B John Pastor, 1917

William's memoirs are taken from this book.

The Voluntary Principle, The Religion of the Bible and A Blessing in the World by William Hopcraft. 1836

Voluntaryism (That Curse on Good Government) Disproved from Scripture and Experience By T. H., 1836

Weekly Dispatch (London), March 12th 1826

About the Author

Catherine Green is an established freelance writer. She has been published in many national magazines and has ghostwritten several memoir books.

As a committed Christian, her writing is inspired by God and powered by faith. Her heart's desire is to spread God's word.

www.ingramcontent.com/pod-product-compliance
Lightning Source LLC
Chambersburg PA
CBHW030303100526
44590CB00012B/499